BEFORE YOU QUIT

WHEN MINISTRY IS NOT WHAT YOU THOUGHT

Blaine Allen

kregel
PUBLICATIONS

Grand Rapids, MI 49501

To my Debbie

whose love for me
encourages, encourages, and encourages

and whose presence is more precious
than life itself

Before You Quit: When Ministry Is Not What You Thought

© 2001 by Blaine Allen

Published by Kregel Publications, a division of Kregel, Inc.,
P.O. Box 2607, Grand Rapids, MI 49501. Kregel Publications
provides trusted, biblical publications for Christian growth and
service. For more information about Kregel Publications, visit
our web site: www.kregel.com.

Unless otherwise noted, Scripture quotations are from the
Holy Bible, New International Version®. © 1973, 1978, 1984
by International Bible Society. Used by permission of
Zondervan Publishing House. All rights reserved.

Scripture quotations marked NASB are from the New American Standard Bible. © the Lockman Foundation 1960, 1962,
1963, 1968, 1971, 1972, 1973, 1975, 1977.

Library of Congress Cataloging-in-Publication Data
Allen, Blaine.
    Before you quit: when ministry is not what you thought /
Blaine Allen.
        p.   cm.
    Includes bibliographical references.
    1. Clergy—Job stress. 2. Burn out (Psychology)—
Religious aspects—Christianity. I. Title.
BV4398 .A55   2001   253—dc21   2001029204

ISBN 0-8254-2012-1

Printed in the United States of America

1 2 3 4 5 / 05 04 03 02 01

CONTENTS

INTRODUCTION

"Son, this church ain't big enough for both of
us—and I am not about to leave."

SHE MEANT IT. Thelma was the pillar of First Church, and
she had won the shoot-out with the previous pastor. He resigned.
Only six weeks into my first pastorate, fresh out of seminary, I had
become her next target. It had not crossed my mind that I had crossed
her mind. It was like a story about the wild West. Thelma called me
in and with a wag of her chubby finger informed me, "Either change
your message or change your address." The lady never hesitated a day
in her life, never knew the agony of defeat. What the woman promised, she delivered.

Should I stay for the fight or leave town? I get queasy at the sight of
blood—especially when it's mine.

Ministry. It's nice—is it not?—when it's a suburban, manicured,
quiet, well-kept place to come and wash feet. Nice when there's fruit.
When there's encouragement. When there's hope. When there's appreciation. When there's spiritual hunger. When there's readiness to
change. When there's passion for Christ. When it's yours and God
blesses and blesses and blesses. It's nice, isn't it?

But Main Street in Dodge City at high noon? The mother of all fights? Dragged off by your heels to Boot Hill? Not me. That's not so nice. In seminary, I never had a course in Thelma 101.

Chances are, because you picked up a book titled *Before You Quit: When Ministry Is Not What You Thought,* you, too, missed Thelma 101. Your scenario likely is different—no First Church, no gun-toting matriarch, no "choose you this day whom you will serve"—but the feeling is much the same. The chasm between what you thought ministry would be and what it has become is exceeded only by the gulf between heaven and hell.

You might be a pastor or an associate on a church staff. You might be a missionary. You might be an administrator or on the faculty in a Christian school. You might be a Sunday school teacher, an elder, or a deacon. You might serve on campus or off campus. You might minister to the military or to other cultures. You might work with children, youth, families, or senior adults. Your ministry might reach out to residents in nursing homes. You might be paid for full-time or part-time service. You might serve without any remuneration. But you belong to the Lord—and one thing that is *not* "might be" is *ministry.* You take it seriously—and you hurt. Do you say, "No more"?

Perhaps the issues you face boggle the mind. For instance, Bob and Ellen Hargrave, missionaries in Loglogo, Kenya, requested prayer for Susan, the leader of Christian women in the area and the wife of Daniel, the local medical dresser. Because Daniel's ten-year marriage to Susan had produced no heir, his mother threatened to starve herself unless he took a second wife. Daniel felt compelled to do so. The Hargrave's request? "Pray that God will comfort Susan and that He will continue to use her ministry."[1]

Or maybe your issues are just no fun. Cameron Townsend, founder of Wycliffe Bible Translators, wrote in his first year of overseas ministry in Guatemala: "This afternoon I distributed some tracts and spoke with several, including the mayor. One fellow became real ugly, but a good many listened. At five o'clock I went to have my supper at the hut the believers use as a chapel. After walking over five thousand feet above sea level, I had developed a hearty appetite! But as I waited in the kitchen where my meal was being prepared, I watched an old Indian woman picking lice off the head of her granddaughter and eating the larger ones. I confess that in the homeland I was somewhat of a finicky eater, and this just about did me in."[2]

Regardless of whether what has shaken you is high on someone else's Richter scale, right now it is seismic to you. Your sense of spiritual equilibrium is gone. The house that ministry built crumbles with you inside. You feel disappointment and heartache and might have shed tears. You've reached the point where your future, and possibly that of your family, is up for grabs. What do you do? Is it time to walk away? Is it time to quit? Your contingency plans might even be in the final draft.

The story goes that a group of designers created blueprints for a Vatican office building and submitted them to Pope John XXIII for his approval. The pontiff examined the plans for a few moments and then handed them back with the question, "Are they angels?" Someone had neglected to put in the bathrooms.[3]

You, too, in your pain might have drawn up a fresh set of blueprints for your future. No concrete has been poured, no nails hammered, no two-by-fours measured and cut. You still are not sure whether you will go with them or not. Right now, they are contingency plans, nothing more.

That's good. If there is an oversight, now is the time to find it, not later. Once an idea takes on life, it's often too late to go back and make adjustments. For ministry, including painful ministry, is not about brick and steel but about flesh and blood. Every decision bears eternal ramifications. It might be wise to go ahead with those plans to get out. But then again, it might not.

In *Before You Quit,* I invite you to revisit some truths—truths with which we must make peace before we make any decision. Angels, we are not.

1

EXPECTATIONS
Ministry Hopes

KATIE WOULD NOT SIT DOWN no matter what her kindergarten teacher tried. She and that seat just would not meet. Finally, her teacher demanded, "Katie, why are you so excited today?"

Katie grinned. "My daddy said I could have a horse when I am thirty-five."

Expectations. In ministry, we all have them, do we not? Stalls full of them. And most of the time we get excited about them, too. The new believers. Spiritual growth. Numerical growth. New ministries. Dynamic ministries. Acceptance. Appreciation. Congratulations. Health—years and years of it. Recognition of spiritual gifts. Growing budgets. Growing facilities. Growing salaries. Churches planted. Believers multiplying. Our stables are worthy of Churchill Downs!

Even before there's a single horse.

Teaching math in a public high school for several years gave me an opportunity to meet a sizable cross section of teenagers. One of the most memorable was sixteen-year-old Wendy. This young lady was beside herself upon discovering that I, too, was a believer. Until that time, Wendy had spent all of her student life in private Christian schools. Both she and her mother had prayed that the Lord would give her at least one Christian instructor in this new secular environment. Heaven drafted me.

Grateful. Simply grateful. That was Wendy and her mom.

Then it happened. I had hoped it wouldn't, but it did. A solid B-plus algebra student, Wendy became careless. At first, she neglected daily homework assignments—only one of every six or seven, but a bit unusual for a girl who, for the first four months of school, had missed no assignments. Missed assignments, however, soon became the norm. To make matters worse, what she turned in left something to be desired. I talked to Wendy about it and sent word home to her mother—more than once—to no avail. Things only deteriorated.

When it came time for report cards, it did not take an Einstein to figure out that Wendy's letter grade did not stand for *fine*.

"How can a Christian do this to another believer?" she and her mother wailed. "How could you? Of all the teachers, you were the very last we expected this from."

The real problem? Wendy and her mother had built a stable. Both of them expected preferential treatment from me because I was a *bona fide* believer. But I never promised a horse. It was hard for them to accept that, although I was a fellow saint, as an algebra teacher I was not for sale.

For Sale

"Why have you brought this trouble on your servant? What have I done to displease you that you put the burden of all these people on me?"

—Numbers 11:11

These words were uttered by one who also thought that he saw a For Sale sign—who thought that because he'd been specially selected he'd get preferential treatment. The term *displease* in the original language means "to fail to gain acceptance, to secure approval." Someone thought that he had found favor with God only to have the rug snatched from under his feet.

The someone? Moses. Legendary. Bigger than life. In the wilderness with two to three million people and not a grocery store in sight . . .

and again the Israelites started wailing and said, "If only we had meat to eat! We remember the fish we ate in Egypt at no cost—also

*the cucumbers, melons, leeks, onions and garlic. But now we have
lost our appetite; we never see anything but this manna!"*
—Numbers 11:4–6

What a sight that must have been! Hundreds of thousands of adults
with red, swollen eyes, crying because there was "nothing . . . except
. . . manna." God's people had grown so accustomed to God's blessings that even the miraculous—food where there is no food—failed
to excite them. That's sobering. Like a fungus, ingratitude had in-
fected the camp until both God and His gifts were taken for granted.

And the legend?

"Lord, at the burning bush, did I not submit?"

"Lord, in Egypt, did I not tell Pharaoh exactly what You said?"

"Lord, at the Red Sea, did I not believe when nobody else would?"

"Lord, the golden calf. You remember that don't You, Lord? Did I
not burn with a righteous indignation? And this is my reward for
seeking to please You?"

"Thank You."

A Roll Call of Empty Stables

A principal of an evangelical church school. Diligent. Given
to both spiritual and academic excellence. A leader from
the word *go*. Six months at his new position finds the
church, the school, its finances, and the morale of the people
in fast decline. He fights valiantly, winning key battles for
the school, but where did his diligence get him? Within
two years, "principal-less."

Sharing Christ, singing Christ, giving her all to the Lord.
"An excellent wife, who can find?" (Prov. 31:10 NASB). Her
husband had certainly found one—a modern incarnation
of Proverbs 31. But cut down in her prime? That's what
the widower, a faithful elder, tries to digest.

Four years of Bible school. More years on the tribal mission field. Little food for the family. Little privacy for the couple. Bodies riddled with parasites. In danger of disease. In danger of insurgents. Jesus said, "Go," and they went. What do they have to show for it? No souls for the kingdom. Absolutely none. Not even the slightest hint of buds.

Is it fair?
Does God fleece the sheep?
Do we not deserve better than this?
You've thought it, and so have I. Somewhere on the mind's grassy, rolling hills, we've imagined a herd of thoroughbreds. Kentucky Derby, here we come! You serve God. You serve Him with all of your heart, soul, mind, and strength. The trumpets blare. The race is about to begin. You take hold of your saddle—and there's no horse. What's next? It's no longer unthinkable. Quit.

What is a truth with which we must make peace? Commitment— the choice we made to love and serve our God with all of our heart, soul, mind, and strength.

Heaven's *Webster's*

Unalienable. That's a tough word for an elementary child to write; at least it was a tough word for me. The E's and A's just never ended up in the right place. The teacher said (don't they all say the same thing?), "The dictionary! If you cannot spell it, look it up." But how do I do that if I can't spell it? I never could figure that out, so I never looked it up. And for years I was not only unable to spell it, I also never knew what it meant.

The Declaration of Independence signers wrote: "We hold these truths to be self-evident, that all men are created equal, that they are endowed by their Creator with certain unalienable rights."

The meaning of *unalienable?* "That which cannot be transferred to another; something which cannot be repudiated." According to the Declaration of Independence, humans possess certain rights that are not to be revoked. They are ours for keeps.

Moses did not know of the Declaration of Independence. He had never heard of *unalienable rights*. But he knew what it meant. Some things were his—period. Nontransferable. Irrevocable. Among those rights, a people who were not a burden.

And what had God done? *Laid the burden of all this people* on him—regardless of whether Moses believed it should be otherwise. Something unalienable had been revoked—by no less than God Himself.

Haven't we thought the same thing? A healthy body, a happy home, a satisfying ministry—do we not believe that these things are rightfully ours? Then reality sets in, and we find ourselves saying, "After all of my training, this is what I get? I deserve a better place—much better. How could I be handled like this after I've given, given, and given?"

Fair? No way. Last week's garbage gets better treatment.

The belief? *Unalienableness.* Some things are ours. Irrevocably ours.

And what does Scripture say? When dealing with its own, heaven considers very little off-limits.

Roll Call Continued

> The man unequaled in his generation, "blameless and upright . . . fearing God and turning away from evil"—Job—lost it all (Job 1:8 NASB; also vv. 7–19).

> A gifted communicator, one who was appointed by the Most High to speak before kings—Jeremiah—ridiculed, despised, often left for dead (see Jer. 1:5–10; Lamentations).

> Probably the greatest magnet for crowds outside of Jesus Himself—John the Baptist—separated from his head (see Matt. 3:1–6; 14:1–12).

In Scripture, it's hard to lay hands on anything that heaven considers untouchable. Ministry, abilities, family, health, money, friends—somewhere you can find God treating them all as anything but unalienable. He acts as though they are His to do with as He wants, no questions asked.

I know that.

You know that.

God knows that.

And God doesn't forget it. But we do. Ministry and its breadth, abilities and their effects, health and money and their extents, family and friends—all of them are given to us, in a sense, only as investments. If God chooses to add to the portfolio, praise His name. If God decides to transfer His stock out, to Him be the glory. It's all His to do with as He sees appropriate.

Listen to John the Baptist:

> *"A man can receive only what is given him from heaven."*
>
> —John 3:27

And what was John the Baptist receiving when he said this? A ministry in fast retreat. Jesus was increasing; John was decreasing. That's what God was giving him—less and less. But note: John received it. He knew that God could do with His divine portfolio whatever He wanted, and John didn't say, "That's mine, You can't do that." It was God's, and He could do that.

Maybe we need to grow in receiving what God is giving. If it's more? That we like. If it's less? That's probably one reason you've picked up this book. Either way, we have to let go of the word *unalienable*. It's one term you won't find in heaven's *Webster's*.

Conjured Needs

What is the alternative to relinquishing our hold on unalienable rights? Service. Manipulative service, that is. By means of our commitment, we hope to exert influence, to affect what God chooses to put in and take out of that portfolio. We seek to secure a set of results that we consider to be, if not unalienable, then perhaps negotiable.

How does it work? We love Him with all of our heart, soul, mind, and strength, and we are persuaded that *that* acts like an insurance policy against God's withdrawing from His portfolio. With premiums paid in exemplary service rendered—diligent Bible study, much

prayer, faithful witnessing, liberal giving, long hours, fill in the blank—
we're certain that if we scratch God's back, He, in turn, will massage
ours. By finding favor with God, can we not be assured a ministry
minus disappointment—or at least expect *some* ministry perks?

But as did Moses' ministry, our ministries begin to crumble. God
recalls His portfolio, the market crashes in our faces. But with our
insurance—the kind of service we gave—this should not have happened! We should have been better protected. Much better. We
shouldn't have lost *everything!* Somebody did not honor the terms.
And given that only two parties are involved—God and me (or you)—
it does not take a mental Goliath to figure out who defaulted. Why
shouldn't we quit? If you can't trust God, whom can you trust?

Like most homeowners, my wife and I signed the papers on our house
without our own cash on the barrelhead. We made the down payment,
but the balance had to come through a lending institution. For us to be
able to complete the transaction, we had to take out a mortgage—at the
going interest rate. We had a need that only a lender could meet.

There's a piece of spiritual real estate God wants to purchase. He
made the down payment, but He has a problem: no money for the
balance. Enter His lending institution—you and me—with spiritual
cash. We are able to supply what's necessary for Him to complete the
transaction. We can witness. We can give. We can teach. God now
has cash on the barrelhead. He had a need, a need that only you and I
could meet.

Of course, that scenario is anything but orthodox. The Lord is self-
sufficient; He doesn't have needs.

> *"The God who made the world and everything in it is the Lord of*
> *heaven and earth and does not live in temples built by hands. And*
> *he is not served by human hands, as if he needed anything, because*
> *he himself gives all men life and breath and everything else."*
>
> —Acts 17:24–25

Needs? Us, yes; God, no. And since we both know that theologi-
cally this is so, then isn't it also true that He never has needed and
never will need our spiritual cash? In reality, our service can secure

nothing. If we've been using it to meet a need of God, it has been meeting a need that does not exist. And since God has all that He needs, He is not at the mercy of our going interest rate.

He cuts no deals.

He scratches no backs.

He has not been bought.

He will not be bought.

He cannot be bought.

How could God flimflam anyone?

Our Umbilical Cord

As is usually the case, wrong thinking about unalienable rights begins with wrong thinking about God. Where did the missionary get the idea that after a decade on the field he or she had the right to expect more fruit than a few bananas? Wrong thoughts about God.

Where did the wife derive the mind-set that a submissive attitude in ministering to her husband would someday turn him into Chuck Swindoll? Wrong thoughts about God.

Where did the pastor come up with the idea that he needed only to "Preach the Word and they will come"? Wrong thoughts about God.

Works—that poison about which we've warned others yet swallow ourselves. We've become persuaded that we can earn something from our Creator or that we can put God in our debt. But because of who He is—the self-sufficient, great I Am—and because of who we are—the totally dependent for "life and breath and everything else"—if we are going to relate to God at all, it must be through another realm.

How Does One Get into the Family of God?

> *For it is by grace you have been saved, through faith—and this not from yourselves, it is the gift of God—not by works, so that no one can boast.*

> —Ephesians 2:8–9

God, who has saved us and called us to a holy life—not because of anything we have done but because of his own purpose and grace.

—2 Timothy 1:8–9

For all have sinned and fall short of the glory of God, and are justified freely by his grace through the redemption that came by Christ Jesus.

—Romans 3:23–24

How Does One Live in the Family of God?

Therefore, since we have been justified through faith, we have peace with God through our Lord Jesus Christ, through whom we have gained access by faith into this grace in which we now stand.

—Romans 5:1–2

Be on your guard so that you may not be carried away by the error of lawless men and fall from your secure position. But grow in the grace and knowledge of our Lord and Savior Jesus Christ.

—2 Peter 3:17–18

Let us then approach the throne of grace with confidence, so that we may receive mercy and find grace to help us in our time of need.

—Hebrews 4:16

One enters and succeeds in the family of God by His grace. We breathe it. We eat it. We sleep it. It is only because God wants us to do so that we enjoy Him and His goodness. It is all undeserved. We don't earn brownie points. We don't work to be accepted. We work because we *are* accepted. Our obedience is born out of a profound love for God. That's the realm in which we and all of the rest of God's children live—the realm of grace, God's heart of love, displayed at Calvary in the death of His Son on our behalf, extended to us freely, now and forever. Even down to the Bible's very last verse:

The grace of the Lord Jesus be with God's people. Amen.

—Revelation 22:21

That's just the way He is, the God of grace. And it is the only way that He relates to His own. No deals. No back-scratching. No schmoozing. Grace—that's the umbilical cord between God and His people. His grace flows to us, from which flows our service to Him. Everything that we need, God supplies by His grace. Everything that God needs, He is to Himself without any of us.

We may muse, "But what about the gospel—does not God need me to fulfill the Great Commission?" Yes, but only because He has ordained it so. In truth, He is able to accomplish the same job more effectively and a lot more quickly without you or me. "Is anything too hard for the LORD?" (Gen. 18:14).

"But," we might say, "what about our shekels? Doesn't God's kingdom depend on money to operate?" Only in the sense that He has decreed it so. But God doesn't offer a free video if you send $25 or more to help defray monthly bills. God doesn't need your gifts or mine to sustain His ministry. "To the LORD your God belong the heavens, even the highest heavens, the earth and everything in it" (Deut. 10:14). Even a life that is surrendered to Him cannot obligate God, for it is He "who works in you to will and to act according to his good purpose" (Phil. 2:13). Ditto that for prayer and fasting and anything else that we do that is linked to spirituality.

God uses what we have only because that's how He arranged it, not because He lacks something. He never needs to save face. He never is red-faced. He never comes up short. He has not, does not, and will not need our assistance to get Him out of a bind. God—the only self-contained Person in existence—and His grace make any obligation on His part impossible. He is no man's debtor.

Threads in Lieu of Strings

I know very few people who like to go to the dentist—and that includes me. Approaching the appointed hour is like approaching the electric chair. The walk down the corridor. The cell doors slam shut. The inmate is strapped into the chair. The instruments of pain await their master. And then footsteps—footsteps whose claps ricochet down the hall. It's the executioner. "Please, please, you've got the wrong man!"

I just don't like to go to a dentist—with one notable exception.

My brother Dale is a dentist. So is his wife. They have a practice in another state, hundreds of miles from where I live. Regardless of the distance, if I have a dental problem, Dale is without fail the first person I see. Even for a checkup, I want to be under his care. I know that it is better to have a local practitioner, and I do in case of an emergency. But first I have to talk with Dale. Because of Dale, I have no sweaty palms.

And I know why. Dale is six years my junior. In years gone by, when we were both under the same roof, I was the king. He knew his place, and I knew mine. I was the elder brother with all rights pertaining thereto. He was the younger brother, looking up to me, the leader of our little pack. And although Dale is now his own man, he still respects me more than a local dentist would. And when I'm on the wrong side of a drill, any kind of influence beats none.

Rights?

Clout?

Influence?

God is out of our control. He never has been and never will be accountable to us. In fact, our God is accountable to no one. We are at His mercy, not He at ours. That is one of the most unsettling facts about the relationship between Him and us. That's why we keep wanting to bargain. The uneasiness within us drives us back to the negotiating table. Hoping against hope, we attempt to attach strings—or at least a few threads—to the relationship.

"Do you love Me?" the Lord asks.

"Lord, do I love You? You know I love You."

"Do you?"

"You know I do."

"Really love Me?"

"Lord, You know all things. I do love You."

"Then follow Me. You are going to go where you don't want to go. Experience things you wish you did not have to experience. By all these situations you will glorify Me."

"But Lord, what about my neighbor? What's going to happen to him? Are You going to let him off scot-free? If I serve You in the way You want, isn't it only fair that You give us both similar circumstances?"

We're always bargaining, aren't we? Always trying to attach a few threads. They are better than nothing. We want to remove the discomfort. We want to remove the sense that someone else is in complete control. Anything but to be totally at the mercy of another.

But the Other says, "If he never has family problems, health disorders, ministry heartache, financial strain, what is that to you? You follow Me."

No bargains.

No horse-trading.

No contracting other terms.

Follow Me.

And the uneasiness? The uneasiness over being at the mercy of Another will haunt us until we see Him face to face. The flesh dislikes the idea of tolerating discomfort. When the flesh hears the drill, any kind of influence beats none.

Reaching Limits

The preceding exchange also occurred between Peter and Jesus. Attempting to increase his comfort index, the apostle tried to bid for something that was not on the auction block: God's glory. Peter was willing that the Lord reveal His majesty through Peter's life as long as it was within the limits agreed upon: "If You do something to me, then You do it to John." But the Lord wouldn't bite: "If I want him to remain alive until I return, what is that to you? You must follow me" (John 21:22).

And Peter did follow. He didn't quit. He stopped the haggling and followed, even to a death that—according to church tradition—glorified his God through crucifixion. Upside down.

And what of Moses?

Of that particular day recorded in Numbers 11, what is said of Peter cannot be said of Moses. He refused to go any farther. Moses had reached the limit as to how far his life would glorify God. He had reached the limit of his bartering. He thought that he had bought God, trafficking His glory, only to quit when confronted with reality: God is not for sale.

Peter made peace with the truth of commitment—that we are to love the Lord our God with all of our heart, soul, mind, and strength. Peter made his peace, a peace that was contingent on his awareness of how the Lord relates to His own—through grace. Moses did not.

And you?

If you want to walk away—maybe even quit for good—because of a disagreement with heaven over who should have done what, then you are doing the same as Moses did. Jesus Christ said, "Follow Me," leaving no room for negotiation. To think that you could buy Him is foolish. To quit as if He had cheated you by breaking some agreement is—well . . . pride in its crudest form.

It means that some things are still unalienable to you.

You believe that God really needs you.

You don't understand the necessity of grace.

Even now you've gone back to the bargaining table, with your last ace up your sleeve: "I'll quit."

Regardless of time and place, we are all human. We all have expectations. We've all been disappointed. No matter the century, many people—including Moses—have felt the pressure to quit, and some of them have buckled.

Was it because they were flimflammed? No. It was lack of commitment. A choice was made with strings attached. Don't *you* get tangled up in them.

2

MINISTRY UNDER SIEGE
Misreading God

IT WAS MUTINY. There is no other way to describe it. Moses and his ministry were under assault. The people under his charge wanted filet mignon. Filet mignon was unavailable. And the young Jewish nation saw to it that Moses heard about it.

> *The rabble with them began to crave other food, and again the Israelites started wailing and said, "If only we had meat to eat! We remember the fish we ate in Egypt at no cost—also the cucumbers, melons, leeks, onions and garlic. But now we have lost our appetite; we never see anything but this manna!"*
>
> —Numbers 11:4–6

In other words, "Something is going to change, and it's not going to be us. Either bounce the menu, or we bounce you."

Been there?

Been treated like that?

Are you there now?

If so, please realize that you are not alone. Take, for example, pastors. Nine out of ten people in vocational pastoral ministry know three or four other pastors who have been forced to leave their positions. One-third of all pastors minister in churches that either fired their previous pastors or forced them to resign. Of all current pastors, 23

percent have been at some time in their ministry life forced out.[1] Of
those who have been forced out, 13 percent were terminated, 29 percent were pressured to resign, and the remaining 58 percent were
forced to resign.[2]

Sixty-two percent of ousted pastors were forced out by a church
that had already, at least once in its past, extended a well-placed foot
of Christian fellowship to another pastor. At least 15 percent of all
U.S. churches have forced out two or more pastors. Ten percent of all
U.S. churches have forced out three or four pastors.[3]

Yes, I know that some among us do things that deserve that well-
placed foot. Yes, I know that we who lead, more than we like to ad-
mit, do stupid things. But in those kinds of numbers? Friend, it is a
jungle out there. *Something is going to change, and it's not going to be us.*

Misreadings

The passage for our evening family Bible story time was Acts 20. I
read:

> *Seated in a window was a young man named Eutychus, who was
> sinking into a deep sleep as Paul talked on and on. When he was
> sound asleep, he fell to the ground from the third story and was
> picked up dead. Paul went down, threw himself on the young man
> and put his arms around him. "Don't be alarmed," he said. "He's
> alive!" . . . The people took the young man home alive and were
> greatly comforted.*
>
> —Acts 20:9–10, 12

We then acted out the scene, emphasizing the truth that nothing is
too hard for God—even raising the dead.

At the close, I quizzed our four-year-old daughter: "Carrie Anne,
what was the most important thing you learned this evening from our
Bible story?" She thought and thought, and then she said, "Close the
window before you go to sleep."

Misunderstanding what God is up to—that happens to a lot of
people. Christians of all ages and levels of maturity have sometimes

missed God's main point—not only in interpreting His Word but also in applying His Word to what they are facing.

For Christian leaders, that possibility of misunderstanding never seems greater than when ministry is under siege. When the bullets fly. When pressure surges—pressure measured in terms of insufficient finances, lack of numerical growth, numerical subtraction, a more dynamic ministry right down the street, criticism whether performed by a surgeon or a butcher—and what God is doing is misread. Something is not as it ought to be, and the word *out* shouts from our hearts.

Moses is a case in point. His people wanted an Outback Steak House. God did not provide an Outback Steak House. Conclusion? *Time to bail out.* And when our ministries are under siege, bailing out looks tempting. But when we are in the bunker, things are not always as they seem.

Misread #1: Silence

James Dobson shared a story he heard about a mother who was sick in bed with the flu. Her daughter wanted so much to be a good nurse, so she fluffed the pillows, brought a magazine for her mom to read, and then surprised her with a cup of tea.

"Why, you're such a sweetheart," the mother said as she drank the tea. "I didn't know you even knew how to make tea."

"Oh, yes," the little girl replied. "I learned by watching you. I put the tea leaves in the pan and then I put in the water, and I boiled it, and then I strained it into a cup. But I couldn't find a strainer, so I used the flyswatter instead."

"You what?" the mother screamed.

The little girl said, "Oh, don't worry, Mom, I didn't use the new flyswatter. I used the old one."[4]

Two . . . not exactly on the same page, much like the two in Numbers 11, with Moses shouting "You what?" at God.

Moses heard the people of every family wailing, each at the entrance to his tent. The LORD became exceedingly angry, and Moses was troubled. He asked the LORD, "Why have you brought this trouble on your servant? What have I done to displease you that you put the burden of all these people on me?"

—Numbers 11:10–11

All of the Israelites were wailing. Grandparents. Mamas and daddies. Singles. Teenagers. Some of them were whimpering. Others were mourning. Many were bawling. Two to three million people, so overcome that they were barely able to hang onto the front flap of their tents. And Moses screamed.

But God? Angry, no question about it. Exceedingly angry, according to the text. But when the tears turned to sobs, not a peep.

Not so just a few verses earlier. When those same people then whined, "Unfair," God beat Moses to the punch. The Bible says,

Now the people complained about their hardships in the hearing of the LORD, and when he heard them his anger was aroused. Then fire from the LORD burned among them and consumed some of the outskirts of the camp.

—Numbers 11:1

God screamed first then.

But not this time. The whining for steaks—nothing. No response. No 911. No fire from heaven. No turn or burn. Nothing. And Moses misread it.

Bob, on staff at a relatively small Bible church, enjoyed his music and youth ministry.[5] He and his wife, Lynda, really loved both the people and the setting. But all that changed when the two discovered that the church's hospitalization insurance policy did not cover maternity patients—a discovery made only after Lynda became pregnant with their first child. The church set up a love-offering fund to help out, but not enough came in within the first few weeks to ease Bob's fears. So Bob began sending out his résumé. Within three months, the couple announced their resignation—"The Lord is leading us to another church"— thinking that the profit from the sale of the house and the increase in salary would cover Junior's arrival.

The house did not sell. For months, Bob made double payments while attempting to support his family at their new ministry. Plus, Lynda had a C-section, and the payments on Junior made the estimate for a natural childbirth look like play money. If they had stayed with the little Bible church, the baby would have cost a grand total of one hundred dollars. As it turned out, that church's hospitalization plan covered everything in case of a cesarean—everything but the deductible.

Did Bob misread God's silence? Was His lack in providing quick up-front cash for a love-offering fund misunderstood by Bob as the Lord's leading them to another church? You be the judge. But one thing is sure—when it happened, I was one grateful dude that it hadn't happened to me.

The best interpreters and the worst interpreters have misread God's silence. Addressing the wicked, the Lord says,

> *"What right have you to recite my laws*
> *or take my covenant on your lips?*
> *You hate my instruction*
> *and cast my words behind you.*
> *When you see a thief, you join with him;*
> *you throw in your lot with adulterers.*
> *You use your mouth for evil*
> *and harness your tongue to deceit.*
> *You speak continually against your brother*
> *and slander your own mother's son.*
> *These things you have done and I kept silent;*
> *you thought I was altogether like you."*
> —Psalm 50:16–21

A misread.

Addressing those who claimed to have a relationship with Him but lived as if He did not exist, the Lord says,

> *"Whom have you so dreaded and feared*
> *that you have been false to me,*
> *and have neither remembered me*
> *nor pondered this in your hearts?*

> *Is it not because I have long been silent*
> *that you do not fear me?"*
>
> —Isaiah 57:11

A misread.

The prophet Habakkuk couldn't understand why God stood around
with His hands in His pockets when obvious wrong took place. He
said to the Lord,

> *Your eyes are too pure to look on evil;*
> *you cannot tolerate wrong.*
> *Why then do you tolerate the treacherous?*
> *Why are you silent while the wicked*
> *swallow up those more righteous than themselves?*
>
> —Habakkuk 1:13

A misread.

When Jesus stood before the religious leaders, just hours before He
was crucified, the Bible says,

> *Then the high priest stood up before them and asked Jesus, "Are*
> *you not going to answer? What is this testimony that these men*
> *are bringing against you?" But Jesus remained silent and gave no*
> *answer.*
>
> —Mark 14:60–61

When the Lord stood before Pilate, Scripture states,

> *The Jews insisted, "We have a law, and according to that law he*
> *must die, because he claimed to be the Son of God." When Pilate*
> *heard this, he was even more afraid, and he went back inside the*
> *palace. "Where do you come from?" he asked Jesus, but Jesus gave*
> *him no answer. "Do you refuse to speak to me?" Pilate said. "Don't*
> *you realize I have power either to free you or to crucify you?"*
>
> —John 19:7–10

Again, a misread.

Heaven's silence is—whether by the wicked, by one who claims a relationship with God, or by a Moses who intensely loves God—misunderstood. And when it is, usually something stupid is done.

Don't forget God's concern: it's more than just *what* happens; it's *when* it happens. Scripture states,

> *But when the time had fully come, God sent his Son. . . .*
>
> —Galatians 4:4

> *After John was put in prison, Jesus went into Galilee, proclaiming the good news of God. "The time has come," he said.*
>
> —Mark 1:14–15

> *And he made known to us the mystery of his will according to his good pleasure, which he purposed in Christ, to be put into effect when the times will have reached their fulfillment.*
>
> —Ephesians 1:9–10

> *For there is one God and one mediator between God and men, the man Christ Jesus, who gave himself as a ransom for all men—the testimony given in its proper time.*
>
> —1 Timothy 2:5–6

When the time had fully come . . . the time has come . . . when the times will have reached their fulfillment . . . given in its proper time—all of these phrases tell us that to God not only *what* happens but also *when* it happens is crucial.

A man asked the Lord, "How much is a million dollars to You?" The Lord said, "It is but a penny." The man then asked, "How long is a million years to You?" The Lord replied, "It is but a second."

"God, could You please give me a penny?"

"Sure, just a second."

Timing is more important than time. As the coach of Providence, God's interest is not only in the play but also in the development of the play. He is the God of Romans 8:28. He actively causes *all* things to work together. And if the timing is not right, *all things,* including His silence, might be the very things that we thought should have taken place.

Mrs. Paul, the choir director for the West Side Baptist Church in Beatrice, Nebraska, along with her daughter Marilyn, the church pianist, was never late for choir practice. To the contrary, both habitually arrived fifteen minutes before the 7:30 P.M. scheduled startup. But not on the evening of March 1. Unknown to her mother, rather than getting ready, Marilyn was catching some Z's. When Marilyn woke up at 7:15, she and Mrs. Paul knew that their perfect attendance record was spoiled. Come 7:30 P.M. this Wednesday night the choir director and the church pianist would not be there.

Not necessarily earth shaking except . . . Ladona Vandegrift, a high school sophomore, was having trouble with her homework. Like Mrs. Paul and Marilyn, Ladona knew that practice began promptly, and she always came early. But this evening she was detained by a particularly baffling geometry problem. Royena Estes and her sister Sadie were ready to leave their house on time, but their car wouldn't start. So the two sisters called Ladona and asked her to pick them up. Because Ladona was working on her geometry, the Estes sisters had to wait. Ordinarily, Mrs. Schuster was ten minutes early for choir practice. But on the night of March 1 she was detained at her mother's house. The two were preparing for a later missionary meeting. Herb Kipf was at his own home and would have been early, too. But he needed to write an urgent letter, a letter that he had put off writing for some time. Joyce Black probably would not have been early, but she would have been on time. It was just so cold that evening, she wanted to stay in the house until the last possible minute. So she was late. Harvey Ahl would have been on time, but his wife was out of town. That left him in charge of their two young sons. A friend had invited Harvey and the two boys out to dinner. Engrossed in pleasant conversation, Harvey was late. Lucille Jones and Dorothy Wood were high school girls and lived next door to each other. Lucille was listening to a half-hour radio program that began at seven o'clock. She just had to hear how it ended. Dorothy waited for her. Pastor Klempel and his wife were always on time for choir practice, but not on the evening of March 1. Pastor Klempel's wristwatch—the accuracy of which he was so proud—was five minutes slow that night. The remaining choir members had equally valid excuses. At 7:30 P.M. on Wednesday, March 1, 1950, no one showed up for choir practice at the West Side Baptist Church.

At 7:30 P.M., the basement furnace ignited, setting off a natural gas leak. The furnace blew directly below the choir loft—the empty, and silent, choir loft.[6]

Don't misread God's silence. Don't despise God's silence. Don't assume that because He is not doing what you need done, He is not doing anything.

> *Wait for the Lord;*
>   *be strong and take heart*
>   *and wait for the Lord.*
>   —Psalm 27:14

> *Be still before the Lord and wait patiently for him;*
>   *do not fret when men succeed in their ways,*
>   *when they carry out their wicked schemes.*
>   —Psalm 37:7

> *Wait for the Lord*
>   *and keep his way.*
> *He will exalt you to inherit the land;*
>   *when the wicked are cut off, you will see it.*
>   —Psalm 37:34

We all know that these verses are not a call to unscrew our heads. We all know that God gave us minds so we would think. We all know that *passivity* is a nasty word. But these verses are a reminder that, in these days when everyone is exhorted to be a leader, God doesn't always act on something when we think He ought to. To Him, it's not just *what* happens that is critical but also *when* it happens. Silence from God is often a valid response. Don't misread it.

> *Since ancient times no one has heard,*
> *no ear has perceived,*
> *no eye has seen any God besides you,*
> *who acts on behalf of those who wait for him.*
> —Isaiah 64:4

Misread #2: Miracles

Let's face it—neither you nor I are facing anything that a miracle would not cure. Something supernatural. Some inexplicable blessing. Some result that nobody would ever predict. It doesn't have to rank up there with the parting of the Red Sea—just awesome enough to prove to those whom we lead that God really is using us. There's no problem that a miracle would not fix.

But where's a miracle when you need one? How can you keep shepherding when God isn't using you as a channel for the miraculous? You can't . . . or so thought Moses.

> *Moses heard the people of every family wailing, each at the entrance to his tent. The LORD became exceedingly angry, and Moses was troubled. He asked the LORD, "Why have you brought this trouble on your servant? What have I done to displease you that you put the burden of all these people on me? Did I conceive all these people? Did I give them birth? Why do you tell me to carry them in my arms, as a nurse carries an infant, to the land you promised on oath to their forefathers? Where can I get meat for all these people? They keep wailing to me, 'Give us meat to eat!'"*
> —Numbers 11:10–13

The Israelites wailed, "Miracle, Moses, miracle!"

Have you felt that? The pressure to produce measurable results? Quantitative returns? Ministry payoffs that say, "See, I told you so. God *does* use me; the need has been met"?

But still the sheep bleat, "Miracle, Campus Director, miracle!"

"Miracle, Staff Member, miracle!"

"Miracle, Missionary, miracle!"

"Miracle, Pastor, miracle!"

But where can we get meat for all of these people? They keep wailing to us, "Make a difference, make a difference, make a difference *now!*" How can we stay if we cannot make that difference?

The pressure is there. That might be the reason why vocational ministry is a jungle. The intense pressure to produce, to look like a ministry winner—and at the same time remain orthodox. Pressure could be why those in leadership positions change ministries as often as head coaches change teams in the NFL. "You've got three years to produce. Either take us to the Super Bowl or take your bags to the door."

Everybody wants results—*now*. "Lord, where can I get meat for all these people? They keep wailing, 'Give us meat to eat!'"

The misreading? Miracles. Or rather the *need* for miracles. Simply because miracles are wanted, some people think that miracles are needed.

Suggestion. When your ministry has become reduced to the quest for miracles, ask first one question: Who determined the need? Thirty-four hundred years ago, it was the flock. And God's Spirit at times does use the audience to *discern* needs but not to *define* them. The audience is not sovereign. Eugene H. Peterson stated, "Sometimes I feel like a backwoods fundamentalist or somebody carrying a sign around Times Square that says REPENT. But I've been a pastor for thirty-five years, and I don't trust people one inch in defining what they need. We don't know ourselves."[7] Peterson continued, "For me, being a pastor means being attentive to people. But the minute I start taking my cues from them, I quit being a pastor."[8]

Let's give Moses an A on that one. He knew who had defined meat as a need. He knew who had wheeled out the grills, fired up the charcoal, and then complained, "Where's the beef?"

The congregation defined their want as a nonnegotiable need—a want manufactured as a deficiency. To address synthetic needs is to ignore core needs. But God is concerned with the fundamentals. Moses spells it out well: "He humbled you, causing you to hunger and then feeding you with manna, which neither you nor your fathers had known, to teach you that man does not live on bread

alone but on every word that comes from the mouth of the LORD"
(Deut. 8:3).

Humility. Dependence. Truth. These were the matters that were
utmost to heaven. Meat can never satisfy needs of the heart.

But Israel was concerned about the phantom, the formulated, the
illusionary needs. Those never address core matters. They only create
the illusion that more is needed because when people get all they want,
they think that's not all they need.

The wise leader asks, "Who determined the need?" The church
down the street? The church growth movement? The past, with its
better temple? Pie graph charts? *Forbes* magazine? Statistics on plateaued ministries? Who determined the need? Remember, there is
only one Sovereign. He alone maintains the right to define *needs*.

And what if God decides that what is *wanted* is not what is *needed*?
The servant-leader recognizes two possibilities. Possibility one: God
could still give it. That's what the Lord did for Israel. Read the rest of
Numbers 11. Sometimes God does meet human-defined synthetic
needs as a form of discipline. In other words, just because God gives
what we want doesn't mean that God has blessed us.

Possibility two: God does not respond. That's valid. Ministering
without meat is a valid way to minister. It's tough and sometimes
painful—not only for the flock but also for the shepherd. But a meatless ministry can be an influential ministry.

Jesus once said, "I tell you the truth: Among those born of women
there has not risen anyone greater" (Matt. 11:11). That's some reference on a résumé. About whom was the Lord talking? A man who
never grilled one steak.

> *Then Jesus went back across the Jordan to the place where John had
> been baptizing in the early days. Here he stayed and many people
> came to him. They said, "Though John never performed a miracu-
> lous sign, all that John said about this man was true."*
>
> —John 10:40–41

John the Baptist. No miracle is found in his personnel file under
significant accomplishments. Was there pressure for him to produce miracles?

To prove that he, too, was an authentic, card-carrying prophet? He was, after all, Elijah's heir (see Matt. 17:10–13). From calling fire down from heaven to raising the dead, Elijah did it all. And people came to John, expecting to see it all. Yet, Scripture states, "John never performed a miraculous sign." If there had been just a few miracles, John might have left this earth in a roaring chariot just like his predecessor—and do it with his head! But no miracles. No chariots. And finally, no head. His claim to fame was that *all that John said about this man was true.* And that, friends, is a meatless ministry that could never be more influential—always to tell the truth about Jesus.

Colleague, a miracle might take the heat off for now, but it will never do what you were called to do—ensure that all that you say about this one Person, Jesus Christ, is true. You can do that regardless of whether or not there's a miracle. You can do that even though your followers scream for meat. And if it's God's will that you continue to minister His Name, in His Name, and do it where you are right now, He will bring the meat that is needed to keep you doing it. If it's God's will *not* to undertake the miraculous, and should you lose your ministerial head over it, rest assured that, either here or on the other side, He will take care of that, too.

Your responsibility is to ensure that you continually proclaim Jesus Christ and that, in doing so, all that you say about Him is true. Don't use the lack of miracles as your cue to take your spiritual traveling show somewhere else. That's a misreading. When miracles are wanted, miracles are not always what's needed.

Misread #3: The Unbearable

A magician was working on a cruise ship in the Caribbean. The audience was different each week, so the magician did the same tricks over and over again. There was only one problem. Each week the Captain's parrot saw the shows and began to understand how the magician did the tricks. Once he understood, he started shouting in the middle of the show, "Look, it's not the same hat." "Look, he's hiding the flowers under the table." "Hey, why are all the cards the ace of spades?"

The magician was furious, but he couldn't do anything. The bird was, after all, the Captain's parrot.

One day, the ship had an accident and sank. The magician found himself clinging to a piece of driftwood in the middle of the ocean with—of course—the parrot. They stared at each other with hate in their eyes, but neither uttered a word. This went on for one day, then another, and then another. After a week, the parrot finally said, "Okay, I give up. Where's the boat?"

But we can't produce the boat. We can't even produce the meat. When our backs are against the wall and our critics say, "Do it, and do it *now*," we can't do what only God can do.

But we'll try—and fail. Who, then, would blame us for quitting? Only a fool will try to play God and not quit.

Moses was no fool.

> He asked the LORD, "Why have you brought this trouble on your servant? What have I done to displease you that you put the burden of all these people on me? Did I conceive all these people? Did I give them birth? Why do you tell me to carry them in my arms, as a nurse carries an infant, to the land you promised on oath to their forefathers? Where can I get meat for all these people? They keep wailing to me, 'Give us meat to eat!' I cannot carry all these people by myself; the burden is too heavy for me."
>
> —Numbers 11:11–14

Notice the accusations. Slam. Slam. Slam. The term *conceive*—a common Hebrew expression for becoming pregnant—the term *birth*, and the term *nurse* were all judicial indictments—slams against God's qualifications as a parent. "Order in the court. God, please be seated. You are hereby charged with parental neglect."

So who takes care of the children—the two to three million little urchins—now?

Usually it's the Moses, the leader. That's the one who feels the responsibility to "make it happen." And, as the real Moses found out, "the burden is too heavy." Intolerable. Simply too much. Result? He wants out. He sees the situation as unbearable. A misread.

Do these verses ever haunt you?

> *"Come to me, all you who are weary and burdened, and I will give you rest. Take my yoke upon you and learn from me, for I am gentle and humble in heart, and you will find rest for your souls. For my yoke is easy and my burden is light."*
>
> —Matthew 11:28–30

Our Lord's yoke is to be easy.

Our Lord's burden is to be light.

Two possibilities exist if that is not so for you. Possibility one: the yoke you wear is not His yoke. What you are doing is not what God wants you to do. It might be a good yoke. It might be a ministry yoke that others wear, but it's not the one for you. Maybe God did not mean for you to be on the mission field. Maybe you did misinterpret His will about the pastorate. Maybe He was not the one who called you to serve in a para-church ministry. That's why the yoke is hard. That's why the load is intolerable. Maybe you wear the yoke by default, guilt, or pride. But a yoke that you weren't meant to wear is always an unbearable yoke. It's okay to say, "I was wrong."

Possibility two: The yoke is meant for you, but you are not learning from Christ how to wear it. Jesus says, "Learn from Me." He teaches us how to wear the yoke. He teaches us gentleness. He teaches us humility of heart. In gentleness and humility, rest for the soul is found. If you've determined that you're wearing the right yoke and are pulling His load, but your hide's rubbed raw and you're bleeding, then maybe you have not experienced an increase in gentleness within and heartfelt humility. Even the right yoke, if worn in ignorance, is unbearable.

To learn from Him is to ask for ourselves what Paul prayed for the Ephesians and Colossians:

> *I pray that out of his glorious riches he may strengthen you with power through his Spirit in your inner being, so that Christ may dwell in your hearts through faith.*
>
> —Ephesians 3:16–17

For this reason, since the day we heard about you, we have not stopped praying for you and asking God to fill you with the knowledge of his will through all spiritual wisdom and understanding. And we pray this in order that you may live a life worthy of the Lord and may please him in every way . . . being strengthened with all power according to his glorious might so that you may have great endurance and patience.

—Colossians 1:9–11

Paul says it another way in Philippians 4:13: "I can do everything through him who gives me strength." If you're not feeling His strength, if things are such that the ministry is unbearable, either you're wearing somebody else's yoke or you're wearing your own yoke but you are wearing it unlearned.

Ministry defined as "what God wants me to do," and *unbearable* defined as "the ministry is too much for me" are incompatible concepts. That is not to say that we don't tire. That is not to say that we don't need to get away to regain perspective. That is not to say that we can never leave a hard place. It is to say, though, that God does not use unbearableness to get you to say, "I quit." The testimony of the Spirit, given to all believers, reveals God's gift for prevailing in any situation that's within His will:

The God of peace will soon crush Satan under your feet. The grace of our Lord Jesus be with you.

—Romans 16:20

Grace and peace to you from God our Father and the Lord Jesus Christ.

—1 Corinthians 1:3

The grace of the Lord Jesus be with you.

—1 Corinthians 16:23

Grace and peace to you from God our Father and the Lord Jesus Christ.

—Galatians 1:3

The grace of our Lord Jesus Christ be with your spirit, brothers. Amen.

—Galatians 6:18

Grace and peace to you from God our Father and the Lord Jesus Christ.

—Ephesians 1:2

Grace and peace to you from God our Father and the Lord Jesus Christ.

—Philippians 1:2

The grace of the Lord Jesus Christ be with your spirit. Amen.

—Philippians 4:23

To the holy and faithful brothers in Christ at Colosse: Grace and peace to you from God our Father.

—Colossians 1:2

I, Paul, write this greeting in my own hand. Remember my chains. Grace be with you.

—Colossians 4:18

Paul, Silas and Timothy, To the church of the Thessalonians in God the Father and the Lord Jesus Christ: Grace and peace to you.

—1 Thessalonians 1:1

The grace of our Lord Jesus Christ be with you.

—1 Thessalonians 5:28

Grace and peace to you from God the Father and the Lord Jesus Christ.

—2 Thessalonians 1:2

To Timothy my true son in the faith: Grace, mercy and peace from God the Father and Christ Jesus our Lord.

—1 Timothy 1:2

Grace be with you.

—1 Timothy 6:21

To Timothy, my dear son: Grace, mercy and peace from God the Father and Christ Jesus our Lord.

—2 Timothy 1:2

The Lord be with your spirit. Grace be with you.

—2 Timothy 4:22

To Titus, my true son in our common faith: Grace and peace from God the Father and Christ Jesus our Savior.

—Titus 1:4

Everyone with me sends you greetings. Greet those who love us in the faith. Grace be with you all.

—Titus 3:15

Grace to you and peace from God our Father and the Lord Jesus Christ.

—Philemon 3

The grace of the Lord Jesus Christ be with your spirit.

—Philemon 25

Grace and peace be yours in abundance.

—1 Peter 1:2

Grace and peace be yours in abundance through the knowledge of God and of Jesus our Lord.

—2 Peter 1:2

Grace, mercy and peace from God the Father and from Jesus Christ, the Father's Son.

—2 John 3

John, To the seven churches in the province of Asia: Grace and peace to you from him who is, and who was, and who is to come, and from the seven spirits before his throne.

—Revelation 1:4

The grace of the Lord Jesus be with God's people. Amen.

—Revelation 22:21

Ministry defined as "what God wants you to do" and *unbearable* defined as "the ministry is too much for you" are incompatible concepts. Even the apostle had to eat crow. Paul, at least in one stage of his ministry life, said, "Too much." "There was given me a thorn in my flesh, a messenger of Satan, to torment me. Three times I pleaded with the Lord to take it away from me" (2 Cor. 12:7–8). The thorn was intolerable. Unbearable. Too much. "Hello? Placement office? I would like to activate my file."

But Paul discovered that burdens read as *unbearable* are misreadings. "But he said to me, 'My grace is sufficient for you'" (2 Cor. 12:9). Grace— it's not a general anesthetic but the ability to endure graciously moment by moment. Felt needs—even felt ministry needs—allowed within the providence of God are always tolerable. To use the unbearable as a reason to quit is to deny the sufficiency of that grace. "No temptation has seized you except what is common to man. And God is faithful; he will not let you be tempted beyond what you can bear" (1 Cor. 10:13).

On July 28, 1962, the Mariner I space probe was launched from Cape Canaveral in Florida toward Venus. Its functions were to be the following: After 13 minutes into the flight, a booster engine would give acceleration up to 25,820 miles per hour; after 44 minutes into the flight, 9,800 solar cells would unfold; after 80 days, a computer would calculate the final course corrections; after 100 days, the craft would circle Venus scanning the planet's mysterious cloud shroud. The reality—four minutes after takeoff, Mariner I plunged into the Atlantic. An investigation revealed that when the instructions were fed into the computer, a minus sign was omitted—a minus sign that cost millions.[9]

Do you feel frustrated right now? That's understandable. We all do on occasion. But as a believer, neither you nor I can give in to frustration and say, "I quit!" To do so is to feed data into the God's-Will-for-My-Life computer, omitting a critical sign. It's a sign that could cost both you and me a bunch. This sign reverses everything. The intolerable becomes tolerable. The unlivable becomes livable. To say in frustration, "I'm finished," is to omit the sign—the ever-sufficient grace of God.

As long as God has communicated in His word something that's able to sustain you, something to help you vanquish even that which torments, then the unbearable cannot be read as an automatic permission to leave. If we have been doing God's will—wearing His yoke, actively learning from Him how to wear it—and still plan to quit because the burden is too much, then our felt needs have gotten out of hand. We've assumed the role of a surrogate, trying to make up for God, a role that no amount of grace will help us pull off. So let's back off.

A plaque on the wall of a friend's guesthouse says the following:

> I was regretting the past and fearing the future. Suddenly God was speaking: MY NAME IS "I AM." When you live in the past, with its mistakes and regrets, it is hard. I am not there. MY NAME IS NOT "I WAS." When you live in the future, with its problems and fears, it is hard. I am not there. MY NAME IS NOT "I WILL BE." When you live in this moment, it is not hard. I am here. MY NAME IS "I AM."
>
> —Author Unknown

Grace. His grace. Grace that is Him, grace that is now. It's the sign that you do not want to omit. There has been no parental neglect. Assuming that your obedience is up to speed, what you do not have right now you do not need. Because divine grace is forever sufficient, God is not using the unbearable to communicate to you, "Quit."

So be careful. Misunderstanding what God's up to happens to a lot of people, including us. When ministry is under siege, things are not always as they seem. When ministry is under siege, the potential to misread God's intent is probably never greater. To misread, as did Moses, God's silence, the lack of miracles and the sense of the unbearable can lead you to jump.

You don't want to do that. Your parachute just might not open.

3

UNSAVORY ROOTS
A Credible Cause for Trouble

A LADY BROUGHT HER dog to the veterinarian and placed him on the table. "Doctor, my dog is sick; can you do something?"

The vet looked at the dog. "Ma'am, I don't think your dog is sick; I think he is dead."

"No, that just can't be. Check closely."

The vet did. He brought a cat into the room. Nothing. He put the cat up to the dog's face. Nothing. He slowly dragged the cat across the dog's fur. Nothing.

"Ma'am, I am really sorry, but your dog is dead."

Finally, accepting reality, the lady quietly asked, "How much do I owe you?"

"Two hundred and fifty dollars" said the vet.

"Two hundred and fifty dollars!" exclaimed the woman. "Why so much to examine a dead dog?"

"Fifty dollars for the office visit," said the vet, "and two hundred dollars for the CAT scan."

Bad, I know. But you've had a sick pup for a ministry, haven't you? Something is not right and you know it. Maybe there's tension. Maybe there's strife. And, more times than not, maybe money is tight. The legitimate needs of the ministry, which require shekels, are just not getting met. Who wouldn't want to go to the shelter and look for a new puppy?

My pup was sick—very sick—on that black day in the Allen annals, March 1. I was director of a small faith ministry, and my family and I did not always have more than enough, but we always had enough. On March 1, when the rent was due on our flat, we did not have enough. The money was not there. I had seen the ministry's figures toward the end of February, and the ministry did not have enough to write us a check for the fully allotted amount. In similar situations, though, God had always come through. The ministry always had enough. The family always had enough. Not always with bells and whistles, but both my family and the ministry somehow had enough. Not so that March 1. Neither had enough.

I CAT-scanned the situation every way I knew. It's nice to be called Director. It's nice that the board had a budget. But if the means are not there, the money's not there. And I knew why—the people did not give as they had indicated. And I knew what needed to be done. For the sake of my family, I had to find a better ministry and find it fast. This dog didn't hunt. It was time to find another pup.

Hello? God?

Of course, a small faith ministry and the Allen's personal budget are not the first to face such a situation. Other ministries and other ministers who love God as much as I do, and then some, have faced similar dilemmas. God promises. His children believe. And then God does not provide. It's not something that you stand up and share in a praise service. You struggle just to put it in your diary. But it happens. And if it is any comfort, it has happened to the best of us:

> Now Joshua sent men from Jericho to Ai, which is near Beth Aven to the east of Bethel, and told them, "Go up and spy out the region." So the men went up and spied out Ai. When they returned to Joshua, they said, "Not all the people will have to go up against Ai. Send two or three thousand men to take it and do not weary all the people, for only a few men are there." So about three thousand men went up; but they were routed by the men of Ai, who killed about thirty-six of them. They chased the Israelites from the city

gate as far as the stone quarries and struck them down on the slopes.
At this the hearts of the people melted and became like water. Then
Joshua tore his clothes and fell facedown to the ground before the ark
of the LORD, remaining there till evening. The elders of Israel did
the same, and sprinkled dust on their heads.

—Joshua 7:2–6

A legitimate need that went unmet? God had promised, "No one will be able to stand up against you all the days of your life. As I was with Moses, so I will be with you; I will never leave you nor forsake you" (Josh. 1:5). Joshua believed. With confidence in the Lord, he attacked Ai, dispatching only "two or three thousand men to take it." And God sat back and watched.

On March 1, the small ministry that I headed had a legitimate need. Our family had a legitimate need. It was not a matter of lifestyle; it was a matter of integrity. Funds were not available to honor agreements that had been made in good faith. The apostle Paul instructs us "to lead a quiet life, to mind your own business and to work with your hands . . . so that your daily life may win the respect of outsiders and so that you will not be dependent on anybody" (1 Thess. 4:11–12). Delinquent bills reflect upon the One by whose name we have been called. It is almost impossible to imagine that God would test Christians through overdue obligations. To do that, heaven would have to operate with a double standard.

Scripture says:

> *O taste and see that the Lord is good;*
> *How blessed is the man who takes refuge in Him!*
> *O fear the Lord, you His saints;*
> *For to those who fear Him, there is no want.*
> —Psalm 34:8–9 NASB

> *The Lord is my shepherd,*
> *I shall not want.*
> —Psalm 23:1 NASB

Splendid and majestic is His work;
And His righteousness endures forever.
He has made His wonders to be remembered;
The Lord is gracious and compassionate.
He has given food to those who fear Him.

—Psalm 111:3–5 NASB

The Word indicates that God will meet a legitimate need. On that March 1 we had a legitimate need. And God sat back and watched. Something was wrong. Scripture indicates that God meets His children's needs. There is no want; the child of God has no lack. The ministry has no lack. We might not get all we want because our wants are not always what God wants. But God will see to it that we get all we need. Something is amiss, then, if there is a lack.

The small not-for-profit ministry and my family were His children, and on March 1 we lacked. Guess what Scripture passage I read on the morning of March 2? Not from something that I had chosen but the next section in my systematic reading of the Word. You guessed it—Joshua and his problems as director of a small not-for-profit ministry. What was God saying?

Unrhetorical Questions

Suppose that God is behind your pup's being sick. You have legitimate needs, and they are not being met. The first response, of course, is to call it quits.

"It just didn't work out."

"We gave it our best shot, and things simply did not go our way."

"Since our needs are not met, we have no other choice but to move on."

But you *do* have another choice. Given the premise of legitimate needs, needs that are not being met, your first decision is to ask hard questions.

"Is God saying something to me?"

"Is heaven trying to get my attention?"

"Is this the Lord's way of saying, 'Hold everything; we need to have a talk'?"

We don't like to think in those terms. Where there is a need and a deficit, the tendency is to get busy, make up the difference, and do both while pointing fingers: "Lack of leadership." "No foresight." "Why wasn't the budget cut before we got into this mess?"

Action and investigation are all fine and good. They have their place as long as they are done with integrity and order. But if that's all that is done when legitimate needs go unmet, then we dodge the hard questions. Why did God just sit back and watch? When ministerial families cannot make legitimate ends meet, when churches cannot make pastoral and missions payroll, why doesn't the Lord rise up and demonstrate His faithfulness?

Joshua knew that he had to ask the really tough question: "If God is for us, and we did what He commanded, why did our Commander just stand back when we needed Him most?"

Joshua got his answer. He figured out what God was saying. And for that you and I can be grateful. Because to get that answer, the phases he worked through—although they were spontaneous—offer a way to determine if God has an answer for you and me.

What Is the Point?

When Israel's CEO hit bottom and broke through, he responded immediately—with grief.

> *Then Joshua tore his clothes and fell facedown to the ground before the ark of the LORD, remaining there till evening.*
>
> —Joshua 7:6

Here's a broken man.

Today we do not tear our clothes. Our bodies might not be prostrate on the ground. But if the Lord has ignored a legitimate need, the grief should come with no less intensity. We've said that we are God's. We've said that we are His responsibility. It's His ministry. His family. His job. "If God is for us, who can be against us?" (Rom. 8:31). Anyone, it seems, who has a mind to.

God did not come through. He did not provide. If we don't get humble and ask Him why, then we'll never hear what God wants to say. To think that God goes before you and then to discover that He doesn't unnerves serious saints. We're like the child in a department store who turns up the toy aisle, only to look around moments later to discover mama isn't there. That's trauma. And that's us—all kinds of *what if's* race through our minds. Where is our Parent? Did we make a wrong turn? How soon will we find Him and again enjoy the awareness of His presence? Grief. It's the first response when a child of God believes that he and *Abba* are not in the same aisle.

When something is amiss, our Lord wants us to cry, "Father, where are You?" The quickest way to get an answer from heaven is to miss Him, genuinely to miss the Lord and His care for His own. But so often we don't miss Him. Things go wrong . . . and go wrong . . . and go wrong . . . and all we can think of is, "Let's fix it. Let's send more troops in there. Let's not be so naive with our strategy the next time."

The thought that God's hands are clasped behind His back rather than placed on us, though, is just not entertained. Even with wave after wave of warning, some folks still don't get it:

> *Which of you will listen to this*
> *or pay close attention in time to come?*
> *Who handed Jacob over to become loot,*
> *and Israel to the plunderers?*
> *Was it not the Lord,*
> *against whom we have sinned?*
> *For they would not follow his ways;*
> *they did not obey his law.*
> *So he poured out on them his burning anger,*
> *the violence of war.*
> *It enveloped them in flames, yet they did not understand;*
> *it consumed them, but they did not take it to heart.*
> —Isaiah 42:23–25

When God begins to back off, and we fail to understand—we take no heed when He acts contrary to His normal care for us—we miss heaven's communiqué. But Joshua picked up on it fast. He and God were not in the same aisle. The problem was not with strategy, it was not with troop strength. It had something to do with God—and Joshua knew it.

Again, given the premise of legitimate needs, needs that are not being met, do you grieve at the thought that God stands back? If not, be warned. Our God perseveres. With His own, He will not give up. It is essential that we *understand,* that we take things *to heart.*

When "Why?" Is Okay

Joshua knew that it was time to talk:

> *"Ah, Sovereign LORD, why did you ever bring this people across the Jordan to deliver us into the hands of the Amorites to destroy us? If only we had been content to stay on the other side of the Jordan!"*
> —Joshua 7:7

Why? Who hasn't asked it?

There are, of course, times *not* to ask why. The clay does not interrogate the Potter (see Isa. 29:16; 45:9). Some settings, though, demand that the question be asked—settings in which *not* to ask it proves negligent, settings in which God does not act like God.

"Lord, what's going on?"

"Father, how can this be?"

"My God, what is the meaning of this?"

Questions born not of pride but of grief and brokenness. A feeling of being at a loss. A feeling that, based on promises made by God Himself, what happened shouldn't have happened.

Notice how Joshua addressed God: "Ah, Sovereign Lord, *why?*" He knew where the buck stopped. He understood the identity of the One who "does as he pleases with the powers of heaven and the peoples of the earth" (Dan. 4:35). And he knew that it pleased God not to defend His people. What happened (or did not happen) was no freak occurrence.

Did it "just happen" that you or your ministry came up short? Was your lack in a legitimate area of need simply an oversight? Can it be written off as poor judgment?

All of these are distinct possibilities. Often, we do reap what we've sown in unwise decisions. But at other times, the culprit is more formidable than poor judgment. Perhaps the decision was logical, very reasonable, the same decision that had been made in similar situations in the past. But this time it didn't work. Something—or more precisely, Someone—was missing. God did not bless as He did before. "Unless the LORD builds the house, its builders labor in vain. Unless the LORD watches over the city, the watchmen stand guard in vain" (Ps. 127:1).

When you stand guard and something happens on your shift, something that should not have happened, you can't help but ask, "Where was the One who's suppose to stand guard with me? Why is it that as I build, nothing goes up?" In times of unmet legitimate needs, a believer cannot speak in only human terms: "Bad judgment. We need to plan better." The Almighty is committed to build and to guard what He builds. So for us to see nothing built, much less guarded, and not ask *why* is to insult heaven. It's as if we don't take His commitment seriously.

Backtracking

Joshua knew that. As he grieved, he retraced the stages that had led to his plight. "Ah, Sovereign LORD. . . . If only we had been content to stay on the other side of the Jordan!" (7:7). In other words, "We got into the mess at Ai because, a few weeks before, the people and I chose to cross the River Jordan. If we had stayed where we were, this would not have happened."

So why didn't they stay?

> *Now the Jordan is at flood stage all during harvest. Yet as soon as the priests who carried the ark reached the Jordan and their feet touched the water's edge, the water from upstream stopped flowing. It piled up in a heap a great distance away, at a town called Adam in the vicinity of Zarethan, while the water flowing down to the Sea of the Arabah (the Salt Sea) was completely cut off. So the people crossed over opposite Jericho. The priests who carried the ark of the*

covenant of the LORD *stood firm on dry ground in the middle of the Jordan, while all Israel passed by until the whole nation had completed the crossing on dry ground.*

—Joshua 3:15–17

It's flood season. Not a dam in sight. One moment there's water, another moment there's bottom. Then a dry river bed. What would you do? Exactly what they did. "This is God's doing—let's go!"

The Father's will was clear. Joshua and the people were on Ai's side of the Jordan because God wanted them on Ai's side of the Jordan. Both by a dry river bed and days later by the collapse of Jericho's walls, the Lord had certified His will: "This is the way, walk ye in it." Although in his grief over the defeat at Ai Joshua did not take comfort from that fact, he did reflect on the past. He instinctively retraced recent steps.

When the bottom drops out in the area of unmet needs, it's a good idea to retrace our steps—go back over the path that led to the site of our spiritual cave-in. Can we look back and say with confidence, "To this point I was where God wanted me"? If not, then we need to trace back with an open Bible and a humble heart to the time when we were undoubtedly where God wanted us. Disobedience may have occurred way back along the trail. Not that we're trying to dig up some deep, dark, arcane sign, but we want to make an honest evaluation of our decisions before the Lord and in the light of His Word and wise counsel.

If, however, we can confidently say, "God led me into this unmet need," then God likely is trying to get our attention over something that concerns Him—a matter that has surfaced relatively recently. God does not play games. He does not say, "It's for Me to know and for you to find out." Something is bothering our Lord that He wants to get out on the table. The unmet legitimate need is God's way of saying, "You and I need to have a chat."

When God Talks

And God does talk. Joshua alluded to what Israel's defeat would do for heaven's reputation: "O Lord . . . what then will you do for your own great name?" (Josh. 7:8–9). That's when God spoke up: "The LORD said to Joshua, 'Stand up!'" (v. 10).

The grief that moves us to talk moves us to concern like Joshua's concern: "God, what will this lack do to Your name and its great reputation? What will unbelievers think? What will young believers think? Lord, people identify me with You and Your righteousness. People identified this ministry with You and Your righteousness. What will they think now, after I've repeatedly shared with them 'But our God is always faithful'?"

This concern goes way beyond the subtotals and straight to the bottom line. Up to this point, personal confusion over unmet needs drives our concerns. But now the concern is how unmet needs reflect upon God's character. How can we speak with confidence about the Lord's caring for His own when He stood us up?

We can't. And God knows it. So He speaks. "The LORD said to Joshua, 'Stand up! What are you doing down on your face? Israel has sinned'" (vv. 10–11).

That hurt. "Sin, Lord? Maybe an oversight . . . an act of foolishness, but . . . sin?" That's pride talking. But if we grieve, we want to hear more. We want the specifics.

> *Israel has sinned; they have violated my covenant, which I commanded them to keep. They have taken some of the devoted things; they have stolen, they have lied, they have put them with their own possessions. That is why the Israelites cannot stand against their enemies; they turn their backs and run because they have been made liable to destruction. I will not be with you anymore unless you destroy whatever among you is devoted to destruction.*
>
> —Joshua 7:11–12

"But, Blaine," you say. "God doesn't talk like that today. No voices. No visions. No dreams. God's final word to man is the Word."

Right you are. Because Scripture is His final word to man, we do not have the voices, visions, and dreams that the people of other eras had. But He, unlike any other author, lives—even two thousand years after His work was completed, He lives. And, as the immutable One,

He has not changed. God still speaks in His final Word. An open Bible and an honest desire to learn leads us to the Lord's concerns. In other words, if we listen, He will talk.

On that evening of March 1, after reflecting on Joshua and his problems, I concluded that either God was responding out of character for the first time or another shoe was about to fall. It fell. Several days later, I discovered that a gift had arrived toward the end of February, a gift that covered almost all of the needs. Not all, but almost. It was a regular monthly gift and, if it had been the regular size, would have taken care of everything. But it wasn't. And to complicate matters, for some unexplainable reason, it did not make the books. Under normal procedures, that never would have happened. It should have been recorded February 26, but it was not. February 26. February 26. February 26.

Have you ever been hit by a bolt of spiritual lightning? Boom! I was struck. Like playing back a tape recording, I remembered a lengthy conversation just a few days before—on February 26. While talking about an elder in our congregation—one with whom I disagreed—the conversation turned careless. Before dropping the subject, I had "innocently" poked fun at some of his spiritual decisions, turning the man into the butt of my sarcastic humor. It proved to be not so innocent to God.

"Lord, is that it? That's it, isn't it, Lord? Disagreeing with Your servant is one thing; mocking him is another. I knew better, Lord. But I still did it. Forgive me, Lord. I'm sorry. I know what You say in Your Word: 'Respect those who work hard among you, who are over you in the Lord and who admonish you. Hold them in the highest regard in love because of their work' (1 Thess. 5:12–13)."

All doubt was gone. I knew why we had been left high and dry. The seed of my defeat sprang from unsavory roots, the same root that caused Joshua's troubles—sin in the camp. Within twenty-four hours, an unexpected gift arrived covering all of the needs and a ton more.

Consider Your Ways

Does a wise parent use the same discipline to get the attention of each child? No. Mother and Father know that their children are not the same. Thomas knows more than Ruby and Jeffy; therefore, Thomas is more accountable. When six-year-old Jeffy loses the money that Aunt Pearl gave him for his piggy bank, Mama and Daddy do not make a federal case out of it. They do, though, if college-aged Thomas loses his tuition money through carelessness.

God is wise. He is the very definition of wisdom. He does not discipline all of His children in the same way. For a new Christian, a careless remark about an elder would likely not require stringent discipline. We are not to live in fear that every less-than-perfect act and attitude causes God to "get our attention." As we become spiritually mature, however, when we know better and yet willfully disobey, God steps in. He will not let us go on as if all is well. He loves us too much.

And He knows the best way to attract attention in each individual case. Sometimes His stepping in takes the form of a minor setback; at other times He uses a major problem. The sin with which Joshua needed to contend was not his own. In fact, the guilty person was a man named Achan (see Josh. 7:1). Yet Achan's sin cost the lives of thirty-six fathers and sons, leaving behind widows and grieving parents—not to mention humiliation and razed confidence. The point is that however God chooses to get our attention, it is the best way.

And once God has our attention, the fastest road to recovery is confession. Deal with it and, if possible, make things right. Israel dealt with it. Achan and his family were erased from the camp (see vv. 13–26). I acknowledged my own sin to both the Lord and the person before whom I had ridiculed God's servant.

When troubled times appear, don't look for sin as the first and only root of the difficulty. God's response might have nothing to do with sin. But don't ignore digging up potentially unsavory roots, either. When legitimate needs are not met, the wise cannot help but ask why.

> Now this is what the Lord Almighty says: "Give careful thought to your ways. You have planted much, but have harvested little. You eat, but never have enough. You drink, but never have your

fill. You put on clothes, but are not warm. You earn wages, only to put them in a purse with holes in it." This is what the LORD *Almighty says:* "Give careful thought to your ways."

—Haggai 1:5–7

Enough said?

4

NO DELIGHT, NO GO
Things to Learn When God Blesses Your Problems

THE PRINCIPAL AT A SMALL middle school had a problem. Girls would apply lipstick in the bathroom and then press their lips to the mirror. The result? Lip prints. Before the problem got out of hand, the principal gathered the young ladies and took them to the ladies' room to meet with him and the school custodian. The principal explained that every night the janitor was finding it increasingly difficult to clean the mirror.

"I don't believe you ladies understand what a problem it is for Mr. Jones to wash these mirrors, so I've asked him to show us what it takes."

The custodian took a long-handled brush out of a box, dipped it into the nearest toilet, walked to the mirror and scrubbed clean the lipstick. That was the last day the girls pressed their lips to the mirror.

Whether at a small-town school or a ministry, leadership often means headaches. People don't always do what they should. Whether intentional or unintentional, through ignorance or immaturity, people make messes. And guess who has to keep the mirrors clean?

So we take action. Legitimate concerns always demand a response. Leadership must act before things get out of hand. It might mean displeasing others. It might require saying hard things to others. It might mean biblical discipline of others. We know that God has not called us to make everybody happy. Some people cannot be made to feel good until they first feel bad.

But what if the lipstick will not come off? What if—after much prayer, much reading of the Bible, much leadership—the prints are still there? Others see it. Others know that it should not be so. To do nothing is to say, "I am not taking care of Zion." The leader is then in an unenviable position. He or she has a problem that cannot be solved. He or she has a headache that just will not go away. His or her effectiveness as the leader is called into question.

The leader is not lazy or passive. The leader is proactive, courageous, and wise. But the leader fails. The problem might be with programs; the ministries are just not functioning as they ought. The problem might be relational; some folks simply don't like the leader. The problem might be a matter of comparison; in the eyes of many people, the leader does not match up with his or her predecessor. Whatever the problem, messy lip prints are everywhere. The ministry mirrors are now smeared with lipstick. What does a leader do when the problem won't go away?

Go somewhere else? By now you've read enough of this book to know that quitting is not the first option. Hide your head in the sand? Any leader who does that will either suffocate or get stepped on. Pray? Yes . . . and pray and pray, asking God to reverse matters, to get rid of the lipstick and to get rid of it fast. God could do that. And He might do so. But not always. And that's the point of this chapter: no amount of prayer, fasting, or other spiritual discipline will dissolve some problems. They stay put—with God's blessing.

Okay When It's Not Okay

"There was given me a thorn in my flesh, a messenger of Satan, to torment me. Three times I pleaded with the Lord to take it away from me" (2 Cor. 12:7–8). For three gut-wrenching episodes Paul begged. The apostle, known in the early church for the miraculous, set off sirens in heaven on three separate occasions—one of its own was about to get sucked up. Friend, that is a problem.

No, we don't know what his thorn was. No, we don't know how Satan was doing it. But we do know this: Paul couldn't take it. *Torment*. That's the way the NIV translates his emotional state. The biblical word means "to strike with the fist." Paul was black and blue, an apostle at his wits' end. He prayed, fasted, and did all of the other spiritual disciplines, pleading, "Help me, and help me fast." The man was convinced that if God did not act, he could not minister.

But, as you know, God did not act, and Paul did minister—and more effectively than he ever dreamed!

> But he said to me, "My grace is sufficient for you, for my power is made perfect in weakness." Therefore I will boast all the more gladly about my weaknesses, so that Christ's power may rest on me. That is why, for Christ's sake, I delight in weaknesses, in insults, in hardships, in persecutions, in difficulties. For when I am weak, then I am strong.
>
> —2 Corinthians 12:9–10

The presence of grace was never in question. It was always there because our Lord, the God of grace, was always there. The sufficiency of grace was never the question. The insufficiency was in Paul; he lacked the vision to make the most of the opportunity.

You and I, too, are less than wise if we make a move before we grasp the vision to make the most of our pain. First, define the pain: is it something within your family? Is everybody on board the ministry train, or at least this current ministry? Is the pain caused by something about the ministry itself? A few people (maybe more than a few) don't line up to get your autograph? Could it be a general downturn in results? You've pulled out your hair, attempting to turn things around, and what have you got to show for it? Empty bottles of Rogaine. Define what's turning your insides black and blue. Now ask yourself, "Have I grasped the vision, as Paul did, to make the most of the opportunities?"

Paul hints at how he knew when he'd grasped the vision, when it was safe to move on. It was his attitude toward not only his thorn in the flesh but also anything else in life and ministry that beat him black and blue. The attitude? Delight. "That is why, for Christ's sake, I delight in weaknesses," said Paul. The original word for *delight* means "to think well of," "to be well pleased." We call it contentment. Not dry contentment; sometimes it gets wet from tears. Not safe contentment; sometimes it gets hurt, and hurt badly. But contentment when we're not sure what's going on. Until you and I know inner contentment where we are, we are not ready to leave.

My oldest daughter, when her age was still in the single digits, received the following letter from a missionary pen pal in the Philippines.

> Dear Carrie Anne, Thurs. Sept. 9—We are in Kilonngan now. I am having fun here. I am learning Kankanaey fast! I hope you are having fun. I have a friend here named Irene. We play a game called building body. It's a game where you balance a flip-flop on different parts of your body. My mommy is teaching me school. I am in third grade this year. Robbie is very fun at this age. He is very active. Marty is reading very well. And the pit for our bathroom is done, so all they have to do is put boards on. It is not done yet, so we are using our old one. It is called an out-house. The new one is a modern kind. The old one's boards are getting loose. We just got our electricity about a week ago. Before that we saw by a pressure-lamp at night. In about a week we will go to Manila: because my daddy has meetings. And we will have no school because the books are too heavy to carry. Here are some pictures: clown, dog, ostrich. Your friend, Christy. (Enclosed were the pictures.)

Did you notice how smoothly she glided from Marty and his reading abilities to the pit, both the new one and the old one? And the lighting? And then glided right back into the trip, the clown, the dog, and the ostrich? *Contentment* is like that. Until you and I learn how to glide where we are—whether with a new pit or old pit—we are not ready to leave. Until we can speak of our torment with a gracious matter-of-fact tone, now is not the time to pack the bags.

Read again what Paul said:

> *But he said to me, "My grace is sufficient for you, for my power is made perfect in weakness." Therefore I will boast all the more gladly about my weaknesses, so that Christ's power may rest on me. That*

is why, for Christ's sake, I delight in weaknesses, in insults, in hardships, in persecutions, in difficulties. For when I am weak, then I am strong.

—2 Corinthians 12:9–10

Once Paul discovered the very last thing to be expected with his thorn—contentment—he began to glide, moving in and out of at least five ministry conditions with ease. Each condition is worth our attention.

Where to Glide

In Weakness

Weakness means literally "the lacking of strength." It's like being in an intensive care unit (ICU). You cannot do what needs to be done. You cannot produce results.

Several women were visiting a friend who was bedridden. After a while, they rose to leave and told her, "We will keep you in our prayers."

"Just wash the dishes in the kitchen," the ailing woman said. "I can do my own praying."

It's fine for people to pray for us. The more the merrier. What we need, though, are results—right now. But we can't even get to the kitchen.

That's one of the hardest lessons of leadership—learning to minister from a spiritual ICU where you are incapable of doing a thing. Certainly it's not always like that. But it's like that more than we expect. Vince Lombardi said, "Fatigue makes cowards of us all." So does the lack of support at home, the lack of encouragement among peers, the lack of fruit in ministry, perhaps a physical ailment. And wherever there is a weakness, someone will imagine the worst: "See, I told you so. He's incompetent."

But weakness never rules the one who delights.

In Insults

The word translated *insult* from the original means "an injury," whether verbal or physical. Somebody is just determined to put you down. Somebody is unusually concerned about your demotion. That little light of yours they are going to blow out.

You know what a cannibal's favorite game is? Swallow the leader. And, like it or not, cannibals exist in ministry. Paul had them. The early church had them. Our Lord certainly had them. You and your family will at times be lunch for someone.

A lady was asked, "Has your husband lived up to all the things he said before you were married?"

"No. He's only lived up to one."

"What's that?"

"He said he wasn't good enough for me."

And to some, no matter what or how much you do, you are not good enough and you never will be.

But insults never rule the one who delights.

In Hardship

Distress. Calamity. Reversal. Tragedy. You get the idea. This is no Sunday school picnic that got rained on. This is rough stuff. One of the primary meanings for *hardship* is "in necessity." As you minister for the Lord's sake, you are operating without the necessary and normal tools to get the job done. Hardship. Success has many faces; hardship has only a few. You can see it in your face because it's reflected in the face of your spouse. If you had known before you said *yes,* you never would have come. But you did come, and it's rough. Hardships for Christ's sake.

But hardship never rules the one who delights.

In Persecution

In an interview, Chuck Colson shared the following story. "I recently heard of a Chinese couple who lived through the persecution of Christians during the late fifties. They were told to renounce Christ, but they wouldn't. So their eleven-year-old son was pushed up against a wall by Communist guards and slowly tortured. Finally, they cut out his heart, and handed it to the parents, and said, 'Now will you renounce Christ?' They still said no, they would not. So they were thrown in prison. The only way they could communicate—one was in the men's wing of the prison, the other in the woman's—was to sing gospel songs. Every day, the husband could hear the wife sing, the wife could hear the husband sing. For years, that was the only way they could communicate."[1]

Flung to the lions? Tortured on the rack? Hissing molten lead poured down the back? Body parts cut off and roasted before the eyes? No, especially not in the Western world. You and I do not experience the persecution that others have, and in some countries still do. But a righteous stand may still be costly. You might forfeit a respectable ministry résumé, followers might turn rabid, you might lose the income that supports your family. And if our Lord tarries and our culture continues to decompose, the persecution will become even more pronounced.

But persecution never rules the one who delights.

In Difficulty

Difficulty literally means "narrowness of space." You are compressed, confined. You need elbowroom but you can't get it, breathing room but it's not to be found. *Difficulty* is a catchall . If the preceding four ministry conditions don't squeeze the life out of you, this one will get blood from a turnip. Whatever weaknesses, insults, hardship, and persecution don't do, difficulty will, leaving you in such a state of helplessness that you are finished.

But difficulty never rules the one who delights.

The Glider

It's worth repeating: Paul was convinced that if God did not act, he could not minister. But as you know, God did not act, and Paul did minister—more effectively than he ever dreamed.

But he said to me, "My grace is sufficient for you, for my power is made perfect in weakness." Therefore I will boast all the more gladly about my weaknesses, so that Christ's power may rest on me. That is why, for Christ's sake, I delight in weaknesses, in insults, in hardships, in persecutions, in difficulties. For when I am weak, then I am strong.

—2 Corinthians 12:9–10

If ministry that increases in effectiveness is also our concern, we must let God teach us as He sees fit. Contentment is not *today* minus weakness, insult, hardship, persecution, or difficulty. It is not *today* plus tomorrow's hoped-for blessings, prosperity, and acceptance. Because of His grace, contentment is *today* minus nothing, plus nothing. It is the ability to learn everything that God is teaching in every situation in which He places us. And if, through His strength perfected in us, God intends to make us more effective in the light of eternity, then don't cut class. The Lord said, "Blessed are those who mourn, for they will be comforted" (Matt. 5:4). Mourn the weaknesses, mourn the insults, mourn the hardships, mourn the persecutions, mourn the difficulties. Mourn before the Lord. That's all right. But don't run. Let Him do what He said He would do—comfort. George Bernard Shaw said that there is no satisfaction in hanging a man who does not object to it. When you are comforted, empowered by His strength, your delight will give none of your detractors satisfaction.

May I ask some questions that might help you determine if it's best to leave now where you are or wait—wait maybe for what some would consider a ministerial hanging? Honest answers to these questions might help you decide if you can, with God's blessing, move on from a hard place.

1.   Paul said "When I am weak, then I am strong." In your hard place, do you ever feel strength to minister when there is no strength? In the pulpit (when you know before you step in it that your spiritual gauge is on empty), in a meeting (when you know before it's called to order that someone wants an autopsy done on you), with your family (when you know that you long

for solitude)—do you find yourself inexplicably empowered? Where once you felt lacking—like the tin man, the lion, and the scarecrow from *The Wizard of Oz*—did you become infused with heart, courage, and mental freshness as you began to serve? When you minister, does a transformation ever take place that catches even you off guard? If not, then you probably have no business leaving until you figure out why God's not doing for you what He did for Paul and others who have caught His vision.

> *Do you not know?*
>   *Have you not heard?*
> *The Lord is the everlasting God,*
>   *the Creator of the ends of the earth.*
> *He will not grow tired or weary,*
>   *and his understanding no one can fathom.*
> *He gives strength to the weary*
>   *and increases the power of the weak.*
> *Even youths grow tired and weary,*
>   *and young men stumble and fall;*
> *but those who hope in the Lord*
>   *will renew their strength.*
> *They will soar on wings like eagles;*
>   *they will run and not grow weary,*
>   *they will walk and not be faint.*
>   —Isaiah 40:28–31

2. Paul stated, "I delight in weaknesses, in insults, in hardships, in persecutions, in difficulties." The word *delight* from the original implies a repeatable state. Note that the items on the list of situations that gave Paul the opportunity to delight are in the plural. The question is this: Have you in your hard place felt the infusion of ability to go beyond what you know you can do—felt it not just once or in only one kind of ministry setting but repeatedly in different settings? In public ministry as one to many? In public ministry as one to a few? In private ministry?

In preparing to minister whether to many or to one? Sir Winston Churchill said, "If you have an important point to make, don't try to be subtle or clever. Use a pile driver. Hit the point once. Then come back and hit it again. Then hit it a third time—a tremendous whack." God has an important point to make: authentic power comes through debilitating weakness. And because you and I find that so unbelievable, God will make His point more than once, sometimes with some pretty good whacks. If you've felt infused, if you've felt enabled, repeatedly and in different ministry settings, then you may be a candidate for a change. You are learning what Paul learned:

> *I have learned to be content whatever the circumstances. I know what it is to be in need, and I know what it is to have plenty. I have learned the secret of being content in any and every situation, whether well fed or hungry, whether living in plenty or in want. I can do everything through him who gives me strength.*
>
> —Philippians 4:11–13

3. But Paul took it further than that. He said when he was put to a disadvantage that he would "boast all the more gladly" about the weakness. The word *boast* from the original means "to glory, to be happy about," almost a "bring-it-on" attitude. Third question: not as a masochist, but as one fully confident of God's grace to enable you over and over again, do you have a "bring-it-on" attitude? Are you persuaded that whatever is brought on, you are able, because of God, to more than handle it? Friend, if you can say *yes* to this, it's safe to consider a move. You are running from nothing. With Paul you can say, "I can do everything through him who gives me strength" (Phil. 4:13).

An old hermit in the mountains of Virginia, a gifted old man with a rare ability to see things as they really are, was the butt of many a teenager's sick jokes. One day, several boys decided that they would fool the old man, putting him in a no-win situation. "I'll take a bird in my hand," said one, "hold it so he can recognize it through the cracks of my fingers, and ask him what it is. When he answers, I'll then ask if it is alive or dead. If he says dead, I will let it fly away. If he says alive, I will crush it."

"Old man, old man, what's in my hand?"

"Well, son, it looks like you've caught yourself a bird."

"Old man, tell me now if it's alive or dead?"

With eyes fixed on the teenager like a surgical laser beam, the gentleman answered, "It is as you wish."[2]

Servant of Christ, what is it that you have in your hand? Hope—to do good through your ministry? Dreams—that your ministry will make an eternal difference?

Tell me, is it alive or dead? You think it's over, don't you? More than you can take. Too much. Dead.

It's not. It is as you wish. Open the hand. Capture the vision of Paul. Fly. Soar like the eagle. Your horizon is as great as the will of God.

5

WHO'S CALLING THE SHOTS?

A Refresher on the Sovereignty of God

"WE WERE ON OUR INITIAL trip to visit the Mura-Piraha people in Brazil," Arlo Heinrichs recalls, reminiscing about his early days as a Wycliffe missionary.

> As we sat on the bank, we noticed movement across the river and spotted a dugout canoe coming toward us. It was not our guides [who had gone ahead to find food]. Our hearts started pounding as stories of missionary tragedies flashed across our minds. Those bronze, muscular men made straight for us—never a sign of emotion crossing their faces. They tied their dugout to the end of our launch, walked the length of the boat and came right up close to me. One man broke the silence. Without any indication of his mood on his face, he asked in broken Portuguese, "You have Gillette Blue Blades?"[1]

God is good. He knows that at times we need to revel in a little holy laughter. To loosen up. Relax. And be reminded again that He's still in control. It's a truth that we can take to the bank. Whether it's in South America or South Atlanta, if we are God's child, we sing with the psalmist:

The Lord reigns.
—Psalm 99:1

He is the Lord our God.
—Psalm 105:7

Our God is in heaven;
he does whatever pleases him.
—Psalm 115:3

Amen, amen, and amen! It's a comfortable truth on which to relax and unwind, a settee that's a must for every Christian's parlor. The sovereignty of God—where would we be without it?

But just suppose that those "bronze, muscular men" had not asked for a package of Gillette Blue Blades. Suppose they had brought their own—to shave, to cut, to bleed some red blood. It has happened, you know. Who's boss then?

The tribesmen? The devil? Certainly not the missionaries. Who's calling the shots then, when the unthinkable takes place?

Fuzzy Reception

When you're hurting—whether it's your own blood that's spilled or that of someone you love—and you're ready to give up, it's hard to say, "God is in control." Forget the titles and letters in front of or behind your name. Forget what you've told others in times of need. This is Reverend Us now. This is *our* spiritual angina. The thought of God as sovereign in the context of an unbearable ministry does not set well. With control comes responsibility. Whoever makes the decisions answers for the decisions.

We don't want to claim that everything that happens to us is God's doing. No. We don't want to say that. God might *not* have done it. There's Satan. There's the flesh. Not to mention the world system that is a hothouse for both Satan and the flesh. No, we do not want to say that God does everything.

But do we want to say, then, that some things are out of His control?

Pain operates at will? There's no accountability. No supervision. Things simply must run their course. No. We don't want to say that either.

But when you are hurting and ready to give up, you are sometimes tempted to think it, regardless of what Bible college or seminary you've attended, regardless of how many years you've served the Lord. Pressure squeezes all kinds of thoughts out of us, distorting truths once held orthodox, with divine sovereignty one of the first to blur.

After a full day, I like to kick off my shoes and watch the evening news. To some people it's a bore, but to me it's a form of relaxation. (I know, I need help.) When we lived in Chicago with only a rooftop antenna, there was a minor problem: fuzzy screens. My antenna had an unobstructed line with the television transmission antennae on the Sears tower—except for the American, Delta, United, Air France, British Airways, TWA, Continental, you name it, airlines' flight paths. We lived five minutes from O'Hare, one of the world's busiest airports. Jets do wonders for the traveler but not for my TV screen. Double images. Snowy pictures. Green faces for evening news hosts. The anchors looked like characters from a science fiction thriller!

Were they? Of course not. Reality exists at the original source— the network studios—not after being transmitted through cameras, cables, outer space, and glancing off trees and planes on the way to my television set. The faces on the screen were only representations of TV personalities. Even though I have never seen today's superstars in person, my knowledge of what is true must rule over what I sometimes see on the screen. Where the image is distorted, the problem is with the transmission process, not with the anchor desk.

And so it is with God and His sovereignty. When His reign as Lord of all appears to be qualified—as if some things are out of His control, allowing undesirable forces to achieve their goals—the problem is caused by faulty transmission. Images transmitted through our limited theology and our pain, whatever the type, are the culprits. The static caused by the unexpected produces a distorted picture of God. And usually the greater the hurt, the greater the distortion.

But reality exists at the original source—not after being transmitted through the wounds from the unwanted. If there is distortion, the problem is with transmission, not with the spiritual anchor desk.

Before we say that it's time to quit, we must look at that anchor desk because—and we've heard this before—things are not always as they appear. If we are to make it when our senses tell us we won't, we must embrace even more tightly the truths that we know and even teach.

He Holds the Key

When ministry seems up in the air, spiritual vertigo can plague the best. Your footing is unsure. You lose your balance. In fact, you can wind up black and blue really fast. You need someone to step in and say, "Here! Hold on to this!"

Such was the case for a small group of believers in the Philadelphian church back in the first century. They had been pushed off balance, tumbled, and bruised. Their kitchen was hot with everything in sight in a fast melt, including the saints. Who wouldn't want to quit ministry and run for his life? But God stepped in to steady His people.

> *"To the angel of the church in Philadelphia write: These are the words of him who is holy and true, who holds the key of David. What he opens no one can shut, and what he shuts no one can open. I know your deeds. See, I have placed before you an open door that no one can shut. I know that you have little strength, yet you have kept my word and have not denied my name. I will make those who are of the synagogue of Satan, who claim to be Jews though they are not, but are liars—I will make them come and fall down at your feet and acknowledge that I have loved you. Since you have kept my command to endure patiently, I will also keep you from the hour of trial that is going to come upon the whole world to test those who live on the earth. I am coming soon. Hold on to what you have, so that no one will take your crown."*
>
> —Revelation 3:7–11

After cutting through the interference, what is the report from the heavenly anchor desk? In steadying His people, the Lord makes known at least three facets of His sovereignty. The first element is the most important one: God has the authority to do something about the situation at hand. He "holds the key of David."

It's the King's key. It opens and closes all doors of opportunity. It controls the passageway from one set of circumstances to another. It can change the whole tenor of what you face in your ministry right now. And the authority to use it is His, no one else's. No person. No demon. No angel. No devil. No individual or group of individuals who you think oppose you. It's our Lord's key, and He has the authority to insert it into any lock.

That reality is important for us to remember when we are ready to give up. God has the authority to make a situation different. That's what Job finally realized as he wrestled with his pain: "I know that you can do all things" (42:2). God Himself asked Abraham, "Is anything too hard for the LORD?" (Gen. 18:14). Jeremiah acknowledged, "Ah, Sovereign LORD, you have made the heavens and the earth by your great power and outstretched arm. Nothing is too hard for you" (32:17). And to ensure that Jeremiah really believed that, God later quizzed, "I am the LORD, the God of all mankind. Is anything too hard for me?" (v. 27). Jesus said, "What is impossible with men is possible with God" (Luke 18:27). Throughout His Word, our Lord tells us in different ways and in different settings that there is a key, and it belongs only to Him. Period.

Do you believe that right now? Whatever in ministry is making you ready to give up, are you convinced that He has the key to the very door that would alter your circumstances?

To know that—really know it—does several things. For starters, it discharges high-voltage fear, the *what if's* that interfere with God's transmission. God told Isaiah,

> *"I, even I, am he who comforts you.*
> *Who are you that you fear mortal men,*
> *the sons of men, who are but grass,*
> *that you forget the Lord your Maker,*
> *who stretched out the heavens*
> *and laid the foundations of the earth,*

> *that you live in constant terror every day*
> *because of the wrath of the oppressor,*
> *who is bent on destruction?*
> *For where is the wrath of the oppressor?"*
> —Isaiah 51:12–13

Of what are you afraid right now?

How long have you been frightened by it?

Does it hang like smog over your soul?

If so, then you have forgotten the One who really comforts. You have forgotten the Lord your Maker. You fear someone else. Convinced that the power of the other—human or demonic—has the authority to destroy, you see only one way out: to quit. God's question cuts to the bottom line: "Where is the wrath of the oppressor?"

Where? It's not with whatever would oppress our ministries, otherwise the oppressor would have already used that wrath at will to accomplish his own destructive ends. But that could not happen in Isaiah's times. And it cannot happen in our own times. If forces are bent on our destruction—and they are—those forces do not act at will. Your opposition might think so. Circumstances might testify that it is so. But that's just interference, the "snow" in our TV screens. God says, "Don't forget Me; I am the One who holds the key."

Remember that when you are trying to open a door to change difficult circumstances.

- If my mate were different, then my ministry would be much more effective.
- If Tom and Jim weren't part of the board, the church would flourish.
- If I did not have health problems, we could do much more.
- If he weren't so critical, it would be a joy to minister to him.
- If we had more money, we could accomplish greater things.

Yet none of these things—people, circumstances, or the demonic forces behind them—holds the key. God does. So why get bewildered pushing against the doors to secondary causes to difficulties when they are not the source of the problems? If your mate or the church board changes, if your health or money problems are resolved, if that hypercritical person becomes cooperative, it's because God has made a move. He has inserted the key in the door.

Jesus said it this way, "All authority in heaven and on earth has been given to me" (Matt. 28:18). No one else. Just Him. The key is His. He alone is able to make things different.

Holy, Holy, Holy

"But, Blaine," you say, "He hasn't. Why won't He?"

Wouldn't we both like to know! For sure, it's not because the key is no longer in His possession. Another "for sure" is His use of it—or lack of use of it. There's no mistake. When the church at Philadelphia got its "e-mail" from glory, it read, "These are the words of him who is holy and true, who holds the key of David" (Rev. 3:7).

That's a second facet of God's sovereignty we must remember staring at a fuzzy screen: it's exercised by One whose very essence is holiness. He hasn't yet inserted the key in another door for you because He cannot.

Cannot?

That's right. Cannot. It's impossible for Him to botch things up.

> *"Who among the gods is like you, O Lord?*
> *Who is like you—*
> *majestic in holiness."*
> —Exodus 15:11

> *"Who will not fear you, O Lord,*
> *and bring glory to your name?*
> *For you alone are holy."*
> —Revelation 15:4

> *"Holy, holy, holy is the Lord Almighty."*
> —Isaiah 6:3

Holiness—the one attribute that the Bible most often declares of God. God's holiness is a reality. A God of love minus holiness is at best a celestial marshmallow. A God of wisdom minus holiness, a heavenly schemer; a God of omnipotence minus holiness, a galactic tyrant. And a God who is sovereign but whose essence is not absolute holiness? Well, only one thing about His rule would be consistent—inconsistency; that is, sometimes His sovereign decisions would be right and sometimes they would be wrong.

When the Word says that God is holy, it means that at the very least He is totally incapable of any wrongdoing—a thought of which we humans simply cannot conceive.

Have you ever looked into a pigpen? Slop, mud, manure. Notice any pigs attempting to bolt the pen? Notice how you wanted to bolt? The stench is unbearable. Why do you want to bolt but the pigs don't? They are used to it. It's all they've ever known.

We are used to blunders, slipups, and wrongdoing. It's all we've ever known. And because of that, holiness to us is just the absence of sin and failure in their various degrees. Thus, although the Word makes clear that God is holy, we still think that somehow there is potential for a crack in His character. We carry this itty-bitty fear that God can err—oh, not to the degree that you and I can, but that He nonetheless has a capacity for slipups. He can make a wrong decision. He can goof up when it comes to His key.

We won't say it, of course. We certainly don't teach it. But, when we're hurting, we mope around, and our moping confesses it.

Suppose that you went to a dentist for a root canal—granted, an unpleasant thought, but that's life. He must first numb your mouth. Imagine two hypodermic needles—one crusted with blood lying on white gauze and the other, never used, on the bare tray. Which do you think the dentist would choose to use to put your mouth to sleep?

Neither. Both instruments are defiled, one by blood and the other by the unsterile metal tray. The degree of contamination doesn't matter. Unless the needle is sterilized and maintained in that state, it is of no use to the dentist.

If we think that God's holiness is a matter of degree, our thoughts and our conversations with close friends hint that God made an error in His use of the key. When we secretly believe that God has the potential to err (even though we confess just the opposite by our creeds and statements of faith), when push comes to shove, God can get jostled. He might put the key in the wrong door.

Ask yourself, right where you are in the midst of circumstances you are considering leaving, can you honestly say,

> *"Who among the gods is like you, O Lord?*
> *Who is like you—*
>   *majestic in holiness."*
>   —Exodus 15:11

> *"Who will not fear you, O Lord,*
>   *and bring glory to your name?*
> *For you alone are holy."*
>   —Revelation 15:4

> *"Holy, holy, holy is the Lord Almighty."*
>   —Isaiah 6:3

Do you believe those verses?

Do you mean it?

If not, there's a reason: looking at your fuzzy TV screen, you believe the distortion rather than the reality. Deep down, you believe that God is capable of error—sovereign but sometimes sovereignly wrong.

Answers?

"But," you say, "I have been sinned against in my ministry. If God is incapable of wrong, and wrong has been committed against me, how could He allow it? How can I stay when it seems that wrong means nothing to God?"

Earlier in this chapter, I mentioned that with control comes responsibility; whoever makes the decisions answers for the decisions. If a subordinate creates havoc in an organization, who's held accountable?

The superior who gave that subordinate his freedom. To allow is to be responsible.

Not so with God. You and I, though tempted to do so, cannot apply to the eternal One the assumptions accepted in our time and space. Our Lord does control all, yet He does not bear the responsibility for all. James writes, "Every good . . . gift is from [Him]" (James 1:17). Every not-so-good gift He rules over without implicating Himself.

Who nailed the Son of God to the cross two thousand years ago? The early church certainly knew when they prayed,

> "Indeed Herod and Pontius Pilate met together with the Gentiles and the people of Israel in this city to conspire against your holy servant Jesus, whom you anointed. They did what your power and will had decided beforehand should happen."
>
> —Acts 4:27–28

Who crucified Jesus? Herod, Pontius Pilate, the Gentiles, the people of Israel, and God. He orchestrated the whole event. In the Father's exercise of His sovereignty, He predestined the complete affair—and it went off like clockwork. Jesus became sin for us that we by faith might forever become the righteousness of God (remember 2 Cor. 5:21). Yet, who will be held accountable for that day in history? Herod, Pontius Pilate, the Gentiles, and the people of Israel. Are we saying that God causes people to do things and that they have no choice because He decrees it? No. That's the thinking of our finite minds. God has the ability to plan and rule absolutely over every event—whatever His hand and His purpose predestinate—without violating man's freedom to choose (and be held accountable for that choice) and without contaminating Himself with sin. That is how great our God is. He functions outside of our theological boxes.

Remember?

> "But the hand of him who is going to betray me is with mine on the table. The Son of Man will go as it has been decreed, but woe to that man who betrays him."
>
> —Luke 22:21–22

Judas was a critical element in God's sovereign plan for Calvary. It was so designed before creation itself; it was decreed. Yet, God says, "Woe!" to Judas. Why? Because although God maintains sovereignty in all events, each person is accountable for his or her actions. People choose to do wrong. No one is a pawn on some celestial chessboard, caught in a squeeze play. God was able to use Judas for His own purposes but the betrayer cannot point a finger at heaven and say, "I had no choice!" Judas was not a marionette. No wires. No strings. Just Judas. Granted, it's a mystery, but should we be surprised?

> *"As the heavens are higher than the earth,*
> *so are my ways higher than your ways*
> *and my thoughts than your thoughts."*
> —Isaiah 55:9

> *The secret things belong to the LORD our God.*
> —Deuteronomy 29:29

Maybe the *how* of the mystery lies in the fact that God is eternal—beyond time in the ever-present now—whereas we are confined to a dimension characterized by sequential events. Maybe, maybe not. But however it works, Scripture reveals that He is able to control everything—including the bad—while maintaining His holiness. No person will stand before God at the judgment, point a finger at Him, and say, "You bungled the keys." Although God sovereignly rules over the circumstances that we want so badly to escape, He is not to be blamed for them. He controls what other people do to us, what demons do to us, even what our own bodies do to us—and controls it all without compromising His holiness. *Great is the Lord!* What a comfort in ministry when we want to pack it in.

Mission Accomplished

So the key is His. And its use will be commensurate with His holy nature. If He has not used it in your situation as of this moment, it's because of one simple reason: He cannot.

But that's not to say that He will not. The key is not meant to stay in the pocket. It was not meant simply to dangle from a chain. It is designed to be used in the locks of doors.

> *"These are the words of him who is holy and true, who holds the key of David. What he opens no one can shut, and what he shuts no one can open."*
>
> —Revelation 3:7

God opens doors. God shuts doors. The third element of God's sovereignty is that if He opens a door, nobody is going to close it; if He closes a door, no one will be able to open it. God, as the Keeper of the key, will accomplish just what He wants. Nothing will stop Him from doing what He chooses to do. Nothing.

> *"I know that you can do all things;*
> *no plan of yours can be thwarted."*
> —Job 42:2

> *But the plans of the Lord stand firm forever,*
> *the purposes of his heart through all generations.*
> —Psalm 33:11

> *I cry out to God Most High,*
> *to God, who fulfills his purpose for me.*
> —Psalm 57:2

> *The Lord will fulfill his purpose for me.*
> —Psalm 138:8

> *Many are the plans in a man's heart,*
> *but it is the Lord's purpose that prevails.*
> —Proverbs 19:21

There is no wisdom, no insight, no plan
  that can succeed against the Lord.
                              —Proverbs 21:30

The Lord Almighty has sworn,
  "Surely, as I have planned, so it will be,
    and as I have purposed, so it will stand."
                              —Isaiah 14:24

For the Lord Almighty has purposed, and who can
      thwart him?
  His hand is stretched out, and who can turn it back?
                              —Isaiah 14:27

I make known the end from the beginning,
  from ancient times, what is still to come.
I say: My purpose will stand,
  and I will do all that I please.
                              —Isaiah 46:10

Nothing stops God. No sickness. No opposition. No weakness on our part. No fatigue. No weariness. No sin. Nothing hinders God from doing what He wants to do. He achieves what He sets out to accomplish. Friend, what you and I face now does not thwart God. We'll hear no "Uh-oh! What next?" From us, yes; from Him, no.

We intend for things to run smoothly. Our goal is to go clockwise. We want the good things in life and ministry: health, a happy family, a place of service that prospers, and stable retirement years. But along comes something or someone and things now go in the opposite way—counterclockwise. It all works against us. Sickness. Family problems. Job insecurity. A ministry that is up for grabs. The golden years turned rancid.

And what does God do? He takes the clockwise and counterclockwise motions, and like the meshing of two gears behind the face of a grandfather clock, He makes them display time. Perfect time. Though the gears go in opposite directions, both are used by Him. They turn the hands that tell Heavenly Standard Time. We just don't call it a grandfather clock; we call it Romans 8:28:

> *And we know that in all things God works for the good of those who love him, who have been called according to his purpose.*

If you are ready to give up, don't mentally manipulate the hands of the clock: "Because this thing hinders me from accomplishing God's purposes for my life, it's time for me to quit." The *thing* has not hindered you. It is not hindering you. And as long as God chooses to use that thing, that person, or those results, it will not hinder you. God might use what you're facing to indicate that, indeed, it is time for you to move on. But never think that it's because the gear on His watch is going counterclockwise too fast. His timepiece always tells His time. In the midst of all circumstances, when God says that it's time for the door to open, it opens and stays open. When God says that it's time for the door to close, it closes and stays shut tight. He always accomplishes His purposes.

Blanket Security

Assuming that our difficulties are not the consequences of willful disobedience, there is no way we can be eternally injured in the situation in which we find ourselves. That's not to say that the EXIT door is never an option. It is to say that God's rule—because He holds the key, because He uses it as His holy nature dictates, and because He possesses the ability to make doors stay as He sets them—means we are secure. Eternally secure. Safe. Protected. Beyond irreparable harm.

Our difficult circumstances, then, rather than being a basis for giving up, are in reality a cause for praising Him. The problems that you and I face in our ministry now, although painful, are themselves servants of a holy, sovereign God. The notion that hostile persons or gut-wrenching circumstances are ultimately damaging is nothing more than a notion, not a fact. Nothing can prevent God from being a perfect God to you and me right now, right where we are. As the eternal Holy One, He's in control.

May I make a suggestion? It could help you with any lingering doubt as to whether you believe, in spite of what you see, that He is in control. It will take faith—but that is what pleases God, isn't it?

Look up Psalm 59:9–11. The passage won't tell you whether to stay or leave. You won't hear bells. No lightning reeling down your spine. You'll just see one saint in trouble showing us other saints in trouble how to pray.

Did you read it?

Did you catch the first half of verse 11?

All the major translations convey the same idea. If you can pray now . . .

"Lord, don't slay them . . ."

—whatever *them* is for you—

". . . lest I forget . . ."

then you are all right. It's another way to say, "I believe You are in control. It's Your key. Because You are holy, You will use it correctly. I'm so convinced of Your control that I'm willing for You to continue using what I want to give up on. Nothing can thwart Your purposes for my life."

The person who can say that is persuaded that God is sovereign, that He does no wrong; He cannot do wrong. And the wrong done by others He works to that person's eternal good and His own eternal glory.

Maybe God will slay them. Maybe not. But the choice is His. That, dear friend, is taking comfort in the sovereignty of God.

6

DRESSED TO KILL
Prepare for Spiritual Warfare

WHAT IS THE MARK OF A good Italian meal? That's what my wife and I intended to find out from friends who had invited us for dinner one January evening. Chefs they were not, but because they wandered like gypsies from one continent to the next, our hosts were the next best thing to pundits on international cuisine. To us, theirs was the last word on fine foods—especially those of the free variety.

After we sat down at the table, I offered thanks. Only a few bites into my salad, I spotted the lettuce on the move in my bowl. There was no mistake. More was in that dish than what I had intended to thank the Lord for. I flipped some greenery around with my fork. Nothing. Did it again. Nothing. I glanced around to see if there was any hesitation by others to partake of that which was in question. Absolutely none.

Then I saw it—or them. Bugs. Tiny black bugs. Enough bugs to justify calling the Orkin man. What could I do? I had just complimented the hostess on how delicious the salad was, and now I could barely finish what was in my mouth! It was hard to tell whether I had just chomped down on bacon bits or . . .

It was all so crunchy.

Heavyweight Foe

When it comes to ministry, do you wonder into what you've sunk your teeth? Prospects at first looked really good—salad green. Lush salad green. Words could not describe your gratitude to the Lord. Not so now. Originally, you were confident: "This is God." Now you wonder, "Where is God?"

Is it getting harder and harder to attribute what happens to heaven—much less give thanks for it? Are there too many unexplained events—the kind that cannot be ignored? Maybe you sense suspicious movement, as if your surroundings are on the crawl. Families squirming. Board members squirming. A church squirming. Things once in a relative state of calm are now crawling with trouble. If so, maybe you've bitten into more than bacon bits. Not bugs, but invisible pests that seek to spoil God's best for us.

And what are these hidden creatures? A kingdom. An awesome kingdom. One that is ruled by the cruelest king of all:

> *Finally, be strong in the Lord and in his mighty power. Put on the full armor of God so that you can take your stand against the devil's schemes. For our struggle is not against flesh and blood, but against the rulers, against the authorities, against the powers of this dark world and against the spiritual forces of evil in the heavenly realms.*
> —Ephesians 6:10–12

Is it not possible that what's spoiling the meal can be traced to that cruelest of kings? No sooner do you stomp on one pest than another crawls out from beneath the tablecloth. Things that do not honor the Lord happen in rapid succession and with such a vengeance that you hardly have time to catch your breath. It's out of control. Forces are out to destroy your children, your marriage, your ministry, and, if they could, your life.

Who wouldn't want to quit? You might be in a full fifteen-round bout and not know it. You heard no bell. You saw no gloves. But now, on the mat, you wonder if it's not best to stay down for the count.

Is that you?

If so, the stakes are higher than you first thought. Sometimes, ignorance might be bliss, but in spiritual conflict it's lethal. It's not enough to know and teach that Satan is an evil spiritual being with a personality, a will, and extraordinary power. It's not enough to realize that as God's highest created being, fallen from his original state, Satan is now bent on neutralizing all that is identified with our Lord. Holding to and teaching the truths that all biblically literate Christians believe does not make us aware of their implications. To think so is to be like Peter. He heard, "Get thee behind me, Satan," stunned to realize how much mileage the enemy had gained without his awareness.

You and I, like Peter, deal with a schemer. Right now as you read this, he's implementing plans to ensure your inept response. You say, "Oh, I already know this stuff. I've taught it so many times, I can do it in my sleep. I have read the books, gone to the seminars. I know all about spiritual warfare."

Friend, the schemer is sharp. Let's give credit where credit is due. His IQ is not that of a potted plant. Outside of heaven, his is the greatest empire ever! If he took on the Son of God without fear and trembling, why not you and me, if for no more than sport? Surviving spiritual warfare takes more than an intellectual management of spiritual facts.

No Calling Cards

The first thing in the morning, my daughter Carrie Anne shouted, "Daddy, my wall is wet." I groaned. It had rained steadily through the night, so I climbed into the attic. I spotted the drips coming off a rafter. I caught the water in a bucket, and then I crept out onto the roof in the cold and rain and patched the felonious spot with pitch.

"Daddy, my wall is wet," she complained a week later. Again? I checked in the attic and, sure enough, water stood in the same place where it had the week before. I returned my bucket, studied the rafter, and figured out why there was still a leak. The drips had trickled down from the top side of the rafter—the hole was really a couple of feet upstream from where I had thought. Out came the pitch. Onto the roof. That hole was history.

"Daddy, my wall is wet." I'd suffered borderline pneumonia. A twisted back. Been forced to apply a fresh coat of paint—all consequences of a leaky roof. And for naught. Tears don't come easily to me, but they almost came that day. How could the wall be wet again? The roofer found out why.

"Mr. Allen, the water ran under the shingles before it found a crack in the wood. From there it traveled down the rafter. The hole is a good twelve feet from where you saw the drips."

A front—the drips had been merely a front. I had made decisions based on the water I'd seen, not the origin of the problem. Energy, time, pain, and money—all invested in a decoy leak. I had focused my struggle in the wrong place.

And so do we all.

Wanting to leave a difficult situation is likely forgetting that "our struggle is not against flesh and blood" (Eph. 6:12). It's overlooking the origin of the trouble.

It's not your campus director.

It's not the chairman of your deacon board.

It's not your mate.

It's not your teenager.

It's not your coworkers in ministry.

Those are fronts. Decoys. Cover-ups. Although we see and feel the drips, that is not the site of our real struggle. Yet, the devil will use these and other things as come-ons to throw us off.

He works incognito. That's his tactic. For Satan, the scheme has seldom failed. No fingerprints. No forwarding address. No calling cards. Just get the job done "clean." Whatever it takes to steer our minds away from the Lord and himself, Satan will use. And the effect? What determines our decisions are the drips, not the real leak.

What would you identify right now as the cause of your discomfort? What thing, person, or persons have led you to think seriously about moving on? Have you honestly entertained the possibility that your real problem might lie elsewhere?

"Blaine," you ask, "are you suggesting that behind every ministry hiccup a demon lurks?"

Of course not. Much of the adversity we encounter occurs without Satan or his vassals turning a hand. We cause many of our own problems through our own foolishness or as the consequence of living life in the nasty here and now. But let's not unscrew our heads and stick them under the pews. Satan can and will do a number on us when we least expect it. Taking advantage of a bad situation, he will attempt to make it worse and do it in such a way that we'll think he's not even there.

Incognito. Don't forget—that's his mode of operation. Remember where the real battle lines are.

Running a Systems Check

Because anonymity is Satan's *modus operandi*, Paul reminds us, "Therefore put on the full armor of God" (Eph. 6:13):

- the belt of truth,
- the breastplate of righteousness,
- feet fitted with the readiness that comes from the gospel of peace,
- the shield of faith,
- the helmet of salvation, and
- the sword of the Spirit.

A deceitful enemy who veils himself behind Mr. and Mrs. Ministered-To will bludgeon a servant called of God unless all of the equipment is in use. If a Roman soldier in Paul's day expected to make it through a battle, he needed all of his armor. If you and I expect to make it through life's battle, we need all of God's armor. In fact, the extent to which you and I take seriously the armor of God is the extent to which we believe that Satan could be pulling a few strings—not just in the past or sometime in the future, but right now.

But take heart. Satan will not whip us—unless we are disarmed. Wanting to quit now could be a hint that we are disarmed. Given Satan's hell-bent drive to see his will done on earth, a systems check is done in order to ensure that we are not disarmed.

*In the midst of the circumstances you want to leave, are
you truthful?*

The apostle writes, "Stand firm then, with the belt of truth buckled
around your waist" (Eph. 6:14). God wants us to believe what is true.
Satan wants us to believe what is false.

- It doesn't really matter what I watch on TV; my time is my
  own.
- What I put on or leave off of my 1040 form is irrelevant; I'm
  not into legalism.
- I need to pad my convention expense report; gasoline went up
  forty cents last month!

"Blaine," you ask, "what in the world do these small matters have
to do with my ministry and with deciding if it is time to quit?" The
same thing that a little cancer has to do with your body—a little here,
a little there, and it will metastasize.

> *Surely you [Lord] desire truth in the inner parts.*
> —Psalm 51:6

> *The Lord is near to all who call on him,
> to all who call on him in truth.*
> —Psalm 145:18

> *Buy the truth and do not sell it.*
> —Proverbs 23:23

Because you want God's best, because you want the Lord's nearness, it is essential that you value truth in all spheres of life. If you
don't, Satan has hit pay dirt. He's discovered a chink in your armor:
you will willingly believe a lie. Truthfulness is not important to you.
He can plant a lie and get away with it. His planted lie takes root. It
grows. Your spiritual senses atrophy. Your decision-making process
has been overrun. And when the time comes for a critical decision,

guess what? His influence is present, and you make wrong choices without having a hint that he's even been around.

Don't buy into one Sunday-school boy's philosophy: "Yes, lying is an abomination unto the Lord, but a very present help in time of trouble." Don't make a move unless you can say, "I've been truthful."

Do you now do what is right as opposed to what is wrong?

Paul said, "Stand firm then . . . with the breastplate of righteousness in place" (Eph. 6:14). Does that describe you in your current life and ministry? The apostle wrote the Corinthians, "For we are taking pains to do what is right, not only in the eyes of the Lord but also in the eyes of men" (2 Cor. 8:21). Can you say that, too?

Satan hopes not. Righteousness shuts Satan down. Two thousand years ago, Paul called righteousness a breastplate, much like the type that girded the Roman soldier, front and back. We might call it a force field. Not that my righteousness could ever protect me from the powers of darkness; God does the protecting. But, as a main line of defense, He uses the righteousness that His Spirit produces daily in the believer's life.

> *The righteousness of the blameless makes a*
> *straight way for them,*
> *but the wicked are brought down by their own*
> *wickedness.*
> *The righteousness of the upright delivers them,*
> *but the unfaithful are trapped by evil desires.*
> —Proverbs 11:5–6

> *Righteousness guards the man of integrity,*
> *but wickedness overthrows the sinner.*
> —Proverbs 13:6

Practical, everyday, every-hour righteousness. Against it, hell's hunter no longer enjoys easy prey.

> *Be self-controlled and alert. Your enemy the devil prowls around like a roaring lion looking for someone to devour. Resist him, standing firm in the faith, because you know that your brothers throughout the world are undergoing the same kind of sufferings.*
>
> —1 Peter 5:8–9

Of course, righteousness is linked to truthfulness. Right is done because right is believed. The two are inseparable. The Roman soldier's breastplate attached to his belt and formed a solid defense against attack. So, too, does righteousness when it is attached to truthfulness. Beliefs always shape actions.

But sometimes we don't realize what we believe unless we take a serious look at what we do, and we might not do that because . . . well, it doesn't seem important. The posted speed limit? Personal calls on company time? Ministry-related expense reports? Television, video, or Internet racy lace? Just a sampling. The point is there are a lot of areas in our lives that we may have accepted as acceptable without giving them much thought when God and His Word—the ultimate truth—say otherwise. To believe what is wrong is to do wrong.

Don't move on to another ministry if your heart has gone to the ballot box and marked wrong over right.

Are you now at peace?

> *Stand firm then . . . with your feet fitted with the readiness that comes from the gospel of peace.*
>
> —Ephesians 6:14–15

Do you belong to the Lord Jesus? Then you have peace with God. "Therefore, since we have been justified through faith, we have peace with God through our Lord Jesus Christ" (Rom. 5:1). No longer are we on opposite sides, He the Sovereign of the kingdom of light and we slaves of the kingdom of darkness. Now we are on the same team. We are friends, not enemies as we were before our salvation. Such will always be the case.

But, in the current situation, do you enjoy the peace of God— peace that is your birthright provided through the gospel—that feeling of certainty, that security beneath your spiritual feet?

> *Do not be anxious about anything, but in everything, by prayer and petition, with thanksgiving, present your requests to God. And the peace of God, which transcends all understanding, will guard your hearts and your minds in Christ Jesus.*
>
> —Philippians 4:6–7

> *Now may the Lord of peace himself give you peace at all times and in every way. The Lord be with all of you.*
>
> —2 Thessalonians 3:16

What is Satan's goal? To fluster you. To ruffle your spiritual feathers. To make you miserable nonstop. Why? Because a preoccupied mind is a diverted mind. Distracted by lesser matters, the spiritual edge goes blunt. The quickness and readiness that comes from the gospel of peace is gone. With a dull spiritual frame of mind, you're liable to do something stupid—like give up on God's will when you are supposed to hang tough.

When your insides are mayhem, your outside needs to stand still. Don't move on without having "your feet fitted with the readiness that comes from the gospel of peace."

What's your level of confidence in God?

As you stand firm, "take up the shield of faith, with which you can extinguish all the flaming arrows of the evil one" (Eph. 6:16). And those flaming arrows will rip through your ministry world.

- Pastor, you just don't meet our needs like Reverend Do-No-Wrong.
- If you were God's choice, God would bless.
- Dad, I'm pregnant.

Those are powerful hits! But with the shield of faith, they are not fatal hits. The Roman soldier carried a leather-covered wooden shield, and he made sure that he always had it in front of him. He felt the jolt, but the shield took the brunt of the enemy's blow. The leather doused the flame. The harm that the enemy intended to inflict was not done. The shield caught the worst of it. Flaming missiles rip through the Roman sky, but the soldier survives!

And so will you. The refusal to panic, persuaded that God is love and expresses only love for His own; knowing that He has not changed although everything around you has changed; believing that He is when it looks as though He is not; convinced that no matter what happens, God actively causes it to work for your good—that's the shield of faith. You feel the jolt, no doubt, but you survive.

> *Those who know your name will trust in you,*
> *for you, Lord, have never forsaken those who seek you.*
> —Psalm 9:10

If, in your circumstances, you've lost that confidence in the Lord, you have no business quitting.

Do you still believe that God will make a difference?

As the believer stands firm, Paul says, "Take the helmet of salvation" (Eph. 6:17). To save means to extricate. Do you maintain that God will deliver you, or has Satan pulled off his goal, making you think that the I AM is now the I WAS? Right now, are you convinced that God has the best possible plan to resolve what you are facing? Are you persuaded that both His method and His timing are perfect? When Paul wrote, "The Lord will rescue me from every evil attack and will bring me safely to his heavenly kingdom. To him be glory for ever and ever" (2 Tim. 4:18), that wasn't just theological gas. Paul expected imminent execution, and tradition holds that Paul was not disappointed—the man lost his head. But God rescued the apostle. By losing his head, he found his eternal home!

The Lord always delivers His own. His deliverance might not be done *how* we want it or *when* we want it, but it will be. Neither you nor I will get to heaven, point a finger at the Lord, and say, "But You didn't rescue me."

The helmet is yours. Pick it up and put it on. To quit without it—thinking that God won't undertake—is to surrender to the enemy in disgrace.

With all that you are facing, are you using the Word?

While wearing the preceding pieces of armor, you must take "the sword of the Spirit, which is the word of God" (Eph. 6:17). It slices away at Satan like nothing else. When we use the Word, we read it, study it, and memorize it. But as with physical food, it's not what we take in but what we assimilate that affects us. We must digest the Word by meditation with the intent to obey. "Lord, in this Scripture,

- what are You telling me about Yourself?"
- what are You telling me about myself?"
- what are You saying should be my response in light of the current situation?"

If your time in the Word leads you to pray and to praise God, then you have meditated with the intent to obey. You are digesting the spiritual food. You can then say, regardless of your circumstances and Satan's use of them, "But God says this!"

Are you wielding the sword of the Spirit? Do you read and digest the Word? Do you pray and praise? Can you look back at what you want so desperately to escape and recall doing that? Are you doing it consistently? Are you doing it now? If not, don't make a move until you value the Spirit's use of His Sword.

Now What?

So that's the armor. How did you do on the spiritual systems check? If I were you, I would not make a change until all of the equipment is on. It might demand a reevaluation of your attitudes and actions. A time of confession might be in order, telling the Lord that you had lost confidence in Him. Whatever else you do, conduct a spiritual systems check before you decide to quit. And . . . well, let's save that for the next chapter.

7

NO FLATS
What to Expect Should You Hang Tough

Belt of truth? Check!
Breastplate of righteousness? Check!
Gospel of peace? Check!
Shield of faith? Check!
Helmet of salvation? Check!
Sword of the Spirit? Check!

ALL DRESSED UP IN OUR armor and we look like fugitives from Camelot! But for astute believers, it's the only wardrobe that gives us a fighting chance.

A dad asked his son what he had studied in Sunday school, and the boy replied, "We learned about how Moses went behind enemy lines to rescue the Jews from the Egyptians. Moses ordered the engineers to build a pontoon bridge. After the people crossed, he sent bombers back to blow up both the bridge and the Egyptian tanks that were following them. And then—"

"Son, did your teacher really tell it like that?"

"No," replied the boy, "but if I told you what he said, you would never believe it!"

Some people would never believe what Paul said either, but it's true. With intent we must outfit ourselves with the armor of God.

But then what? Again, let's read Paul:

Put on the full armor of God so that you can take your stand against the devil's schemes. *For our struggle is not against flesh and blood, but against the rulers, against the authorities, against the powers of this dark world and against the spiritual forces of evil in the heavenly realms. Therefore put on the full armor of God,* so that when the day of evil comes, you may be able to stand your ground, *and after you have done everything,* to stand. Stand firm then, *with the belt of truth buckled around your waist, with the breastplate of righteousness in place, and with your feet fitted with the readiness that comes from the gospel of peace. In addition to all this, take up the shield of faith, with which you can extinguish all the flaming arrows of the evil one. Take the helmet of salvation and the sword of the Spirit, which is the word of God.*

—Ephesians 6:11–17, emphasis added

All dressed up? For what? The threat of combat. And if the worst takes place, an aggressive strategy demands that we "hold the ground!" Because you are outfitted properly, when the evil day comes, unannounced and with a blast, you—criticized, smeared, cheated, sinned against, oppressed, betrayed—can *"take your stand against the devil's schemes. . . . Stand your ground, and after you have done everything, to stand. Stand firm then"* (vv. 11, 13–14). Even the most fertile imagination cannot construe Paul's words to mean *run.*

What did Jesus say when the devil pressed Him continually? "Away from me, Satan!" (Matt. 4:10). How did He handle the Evil One's use of Peter? "Get behind me, Satan!" (16:23). Paul says, "Do not give the devil a foothold" (Eph. 4:27). James writes, "Submit yourselves, then, to God. Resist the devil, and he will flee from you" (James 4:7). Peter likewise tells us, "Be self-controlled and alert. Your enemy the devil prowls around like a roaring lion looking for someone to devour. Resist him" (1 Peter 5:8–9). The apostle John wrote in back-to-back verses, "I write to you, young men, because you have overcome the evil one. . . . I write to you, young men, because you are strong, and the word of God lives in you, and you have overcome the evil one" (1 John 2:13–14).

Could the apostle have written such words if those early Christians had opted for retreat at the first sign of battle? Conquerors is what they were—and, by the grace of God, so are we. What Christ did at Calvary—"having disarmed the powers and authorities, he made a public spectacle of them, triumphing over them by the cross" (Col. 2:15)—makes it possible for us to conquer. We do not run. We might *want* to run. Some people might tell us to run. But we don't. The believer stands firm.

That's not to say that one hangs around for the martyr's crown. At times, those people who opposed the Lord attempted to stone Him, but he "slipped out the back" (see John 8:59; 10:39). Paul often dodged the forces that were out to get him. Remember his nighttime "basket-over-the-wall" strategy (see 2 Cor. 11:33)? Believers are told, "Do not give dogs what is sacred; do not throw your pearls to pigs. If you do, they may trample them under their feet, and then turn and tear you to pieces" (Matt. 7:6). The goal of perseverance is not to spill your guts; the goal is to hold your spiritual ground.

Don't give in to discouragement. Don't leave because you can't hack it. Don't say, "It's no use." If God has placed you there, it is of use. If His pleasure has put you where you are, then you can hack it. You will find the courage necessary for whatever His will should prove to be. And you will do it as a winner.

If God wants to use the forces that are working against you as a way to direct you to other pastures, in His time and in His way He will make that clear. Paul knew when to look for a basket and found one in a heartbeat. And if God wants you to take evasive action, there's a basket ready with your name written all over it.

Just be sure that, whether God wants you to stay or to leave a given situation, Satan isn't the one to flush you out. Don't quit in defeat. Take the heat. You can, by His grace, stand firm. Don't cower.

An Expectation

And what can we count on from Satan as we hold the ground while we wait for further marching orders from God? For starters, we can expect a war of intimidation. *Intimidate* means "to force into action by inducing fear." Satan wants to scare us into disobedience. Nehemiah, under assault through Satan's use of flesh and blood, realized what really was going on: "[Shemaiah] had been hired to intimidate me so that I would commit a sin" (Neh. 6:13). To succumb to intimidation is to succumb to fear, and that always leads to wrong choices.

Is that happening to you now? In the heat of the battle are you scared? If so, know what Satan knows: An intimidated you is a panicked you. "The one means that wins the easiest victory over reason: terror and force." So said one of Satan's most famous parishioners—Adolf Hitler.

But don't forget, if his leash length is intimidation, intimidation is as far as he can go. His tether is taut. He may tease, taunt, and rattle our cages. He may use all types of personalities as force. But if God has stated, "This far and no more," that's all he can do to you. Remember what Jesus told Peter? "Simon, Simon, Satan has asked to sift you as wheat. But I have prayed for you, Simon, that your faith may not fail" (Luke 22:31–32). Satan needs a work permit. Before the devil could crash Peter's party, he needed God's consent.

Satan's intimidation might come from any direction: a harsh letter from someone you thought was a friend; when interceding for people in crisis, an inner voice that says, "You know it won't do any good"; after many years in the ministry, stray thoughts of *What if the gospel really is not so?* It may confront a pastor who's working with his defiant teenager, and hell's wretch hisses, "You will never get him back." It could smother a faithful communicator of truth who's told, "You keep that up, and you will be out on the streets." Maybe it's a missionary's loved one who has a health crisis, and the mind plays out the very worst scenarios.

But the whispers, the thoughts, and the discouraging messages are nothing more than scare tactics. The permit is very clear: "This far and that's it."

Another Expectation

But we don't have firsthand access to those work permits, so we don't know exactly where God has drawn the line. At times, Satan goes further than we could have imagined. What is only a threat to one person turns out to be a 911 call for another. When Peter sat in Herod's slammer, scheduled for execution, it went only that far—just a calendar date—and no more. God's angel yanked Peter off death row (see Acts 12:3–19). But what about the apostle James? Same prison. Same Herod. Same angels. Same God. But James lost his head (see Acts 12:1–2).

Hearts stop. Saints die. Cancer cells multiply. Blood vessels pop. Bodies get impaled on shafts of steering wheels. Planes with believers on board fall out of the sky. Saints lose jobs. Saints lose children. Saints lose mates—to death, affairs, sex, and drugs. Churches split. Today's servants sometimes get "stoned." The worst that Satan can do—and then some—happens to some of God's own children. The Red Sea does not always divide for us—at least not when, where, and how we expect. What are only threats to some people become realities for others.

Why? The reasons are hidden in the wisdom and love of God. Besides, what the world might label a defeat is seldom what God calls a defeat. The cross is forever a reminder that winners do not always look like winners. As Paul wrote (most likely shortly before he was detached from his head),

> *The Lord will rescue me from every evil attack and will bring me safely to his heavenly kingdom. To him be glory for ever and ever. Amen.*
>
> —2 Timothy 4:18

As outfitted soldiers of God, standing firm, we can say the same thing, too, even if it costs us everything. Satan may kill the body, but he cannot touch the soul. He may take all that we *have*, but he cannot have all that we *are*. God's child may lose everything, but he will be known forever as the one who got it all.

When standing firm, expect intimidation. But don't be surprised if there's more.

A Third Expectation

"To be prepared for war is one of the most effectual means of preserving peace." So said George Washington. And it's good advice—

except in spiritual conflict. An armed believer who stands his or her ground will not preserve the peace. A believer of the type described in Ephesians chapter six will draw fire, and, at times, a lot of it. Satan will storm an armor-wearing child of God. His demonic Scuds, flaming missiles that streak through the heart of a ministry, will leave the strongest warrior dazed. Just ask Job. The attacks on him were intense, vehement, and vicious. They were the kind of attacks that you don't forget. He was bombarded by the words of his "friends." His health was taken. His family was pillaged. He faced an intense, vehement, and vicious spiritual blitzkrieg.

We can be grateful that these times are not the norm. Not all strikes are bloodbaths. For most believers, such attacks are few and far between. But they happen, nevertheless, and—with all due respect to Washington—they happen even when we are prepared for war.

It takes your breath, doesn't it? That the enemy of our souls can create such carnage with such precision and with such ease is terrifying! It seems as though there's nothing that he can't do.

But we know that Satan has limits. When it looks as though he doesn't, it's good to be reminded that only God knows all that was, is, will be, could have been, or could be. The devil gains knowledge just as you and I do—by observation. If Satan were omniscient, he never would have rebelled against God (see Isa. 14:12–17), for knowledge of certain defeat and eternal judgment would have made rebellion the epitome of stupidity. Satan is not omnipresent. He has never said to his followers, "Lo, I am with you always—each one of you—even until the end of the age." Satan is not omnipotent. When Job's name came up in heaven, the devil reminded the Lord that He had "put a hedge around him and his household and everything he has" (Job 1:10). Only God can do anything He wants, any time He wants, any way He wants, and anywhere He wants.

So how does the enemy of our souls create such carnage with such precision and do it with limited resources? How does he so easily find our vulnerable spots? How does he know what will make us say, "I have had it; it's time to quit"?

The answer? His subordinates. Remember Paul said that we struggle "against the rulers, against the authorities, against the powers of this dark world and against the spiritual forces of evil in the heavenly realms" (Eph. 6:12). Satan's well-organized kingdom of demons—unclean spirit beings who desire our destruction (see Matt. 17:18; 1 Tim. 4:1–2)—makes him *seem* to be all-knowing, all-present, and all-powerful. With surveillance information in hand, he carries out his God-permitted, well-designed, pinpoint accurate attacks, at times leaving us with a sense of total devastation. When you are standing firm, don't be surprised if Satan tries to gun you down spiritually. He's got the demon power to do it!

The South Side

He's awesome, isn't he? Not equal to God, but no ministry light-weight like you and me either. He can intimidate, even wage savage attacks—if so permitted—applying the mind-boggling forces at his command. In and of ourselves, we could not survive his sneer, much less an all-out assault.

It will take more than armor, more than determination to hold our ground. Something else is mandatory to ensure that we don't comply with the devil's will. It takes what some friends of mine got from Pablo, a perceptive saint: "Lord, when they walk back to their car, may it still be there. And, Lord, don't let them have any flats while they leave the neighborhood."

The day before Thanksgiving, Mark and Blake delivered a basket of food to a family who loved God, who loved God's people, and who loved lost souls in their neighborhood—the south side of Chicago. Gangs. Rapes. Theft. Murder. The worst a world-class city has to offer. The wise person crosses that section of town only if absolutely necessary, and then only in the daytime. And that with no stops.

Such was this family's mission field. But they needed encouragement, and it was Mark and Blake who delivered the turkey and the Thanksgiving basket from our church. After presenting our gift, the two were headed for the door when Pablo stopped them and said, "Let's pray." He thanked God for the food. He thanked God for the church. He thanked God for Mark and Blake. Then he made the two simple requests: "Lord, when they walk back to their car, may it still be there. And, Lord, don't let them have any flats while they leave the neighborhood."

The car was still there. And they made it out of the neighborhood without a flat.

"Blaine," you ask, "did the prayer make that much difference? Wouldn't they have made it anyway without incident?"

I don't know. And frankly, if I'd been there that cold Thanksgiving Eve just before sunset on the south side of Chicago, I would not have wanted to find out. I would have been grateful for that man's prayer. Without it, given Satan's interest, there's no telling what could have happened. Prayer is the "something else" that is necessary to ensure that the devil does not realize his will in our lives.

Paul reminds us,

> *Finally, be strong in the Lord and in his mighty power. Put on the full armor of God so that you can take your stand against the devil's schemes. . . . And pray in the Spirit on all occasions with all kinds of prayers and requests.*
>
> —Ephesians 6:10–11, 18

Speaking for God in the verses just quoted, the apostle reminds us of the centrality of prayer. It's not enough to wear the armor. It's not enough to determine, "I will hold the ground; I'll hang in there." You must also pray—prayer that has as its source the Spirit. Pray that way on all occasions, regardless of whether the battle is hot or not. Include all kinds of prayer—praise, thanksgiving, and petition. And don't stop praying despite weariness, confusion, and discouragement. It's critical if you and I are to stand firm. It's mandatory if we are to stay equipped. Someday it might be just what the tires on your spiritual vehicle need. Maybe even what they need today.

> *Finally, be strong in the Lord and in his mighty power. Put on the full armor of God so that you can take your stand against the devil's schemes. For our struggle is not against flesh and blood, but against the rulers, against the authorities, against the powers of this dark world and against the spiritual forces of evil in the heavenly realms.*

Therefore put on the full armor of God, so that when the day of evil comes, you may be able to stand your ground, and after you have done everything, to stand. Stand firm then, with the belt of truth buckled around your waist, with the breastplate of righteousness in place, and with your feet fitted with the readiness that comes from the gospel of peace. In addition to all this, take up the shield of faith, with which you can extinguish all the flaming arrows of the evil one. Take the helmet of salvation and the sword of the Spirit, which is the word of God. And pray in the Spirit on all occasions with all kinds of prayers and requests.

—Ephesians 6:10–18

8

EMPTY

When You Physically Crash and Burn

THOSE WHO FACE challenges in ministry quickly rediscover some of the church's best-loved verses:

> But thanks be to God, who always leads us in triumphal procession in Christ.
>
> —2 Corinthians 2:14

> I can do everything through him who gives me strength.
>
> —Philippians 4:13

> I have been crucified with Christ and I no longer live, but Christ lives in me. The life I live in the body, I live by faith in the Son of God, who loved me and gave himself for me.
>
> —Galatians 2:20

> Now to him who is able to do immeasurably more than all we ask or imagine, according to his power that is at work within us, to him be glory in the church and in Christ Jesus throughout all generations, for ever and ever! Amen.
>
> —Ephesians 3:20–21

Wow! Look at those words.
Triumphal.
Everything.
Power.
Payload words. Explosive words. Meteoric words. Who doesn't need that in their life and ministry? Ministry life in Christ is not a consolation prize. We have what it takes from within—God Himself—to experience victory in every conceivable struggle.

> *Who shall separate us from the love of Christ? Shall trouble or hardship or persecution or famine or nakedness or danger or sword? . . . No, in all these things we are more than conquerors through him who loved us.*
>
> —Romans 8:35, 37

Thrilling, isn't it? Any demand made upon us is a demand made upon our Lord.

> *Christ in you [is] the hope of glory.*
>
> —Colossians 1:27

Spectacular. Just spectacular.
But we forget—and do we ever forget—the flip side!

> *This treasure [is] in* jars of clay.
>
> —2 Corinthians 4:7

Pots.
Cracked pots.
Faded, chinked, cracked pots.
The implication? Biology is equally in force for both the Christian and the non-Christian, the reverend and the non-reverend, the missionary as well as the local sixty-plus-hour-a-week mechanic. God does not suspend the laws of physiology when Christ comes to live in an individual at the time of the new birth. This side of the grave, once a pot, always a pot. Saved and unsaved, ordained and unordained, full-

time vocational minister and don't-give-a-rip minister—all of us must eat to survive and sleep to function. Jesus, living in a sinless body, became "tired . . . from the journey" (John 4:6). So no matter how many theological degrees are tagged behind our names, we can't push ourselves beyond the reach of natural laws without paying the piper. All of the "Christ in you" verses will not make you more than what our Lord was when He walked this earth.

Spiritual Meltdown

Consider a fellow pot who cracked.

> *Elijah was a man just like us. He prayed earnestly that it would not rain, and it did not rain on the land for three and a half years. Again he prayed, and the heavens gave rain, and the earth produced its crops.*
>
> —James 5:17–18

Quite impressive. But there's more. How's this for a résumé: he conferred with kings without ever an appointment, he terrified local undertakers by the resurrection of at least one of their clients, and he subpoenaed fire from heaven for the court of public opinion.

Elijah—his name connotes ministry at its best. Accolades scattered in both testaments of Scripture cite him as a model for all time. He was God's man with God's message to a pew full of spiritual midgets. What a surprise then to read, "I have had enough, LORD. . . . Take my life; I am no better than my ancestors" (1 Kings 19:4).

Courteous, but firm. Like a surgeon who's done his best to cut out the cancer in his patient, Elijah zealously excised from Israel the prophets of Baal only to face one huge malpractice suit:

> *Now Ahab told Jezebel everything Elijah had done [on Mt. Carmel] and how he had killed all the prophets with the sword. So Jezebel sent a messenger to Elijah to say, "May the gods deal with me, be it ever so severely, if by this time tomorrow I do not make your life like that of one of them." Elijah was afraid and ran for his life. When he came*

*to Beersheba in Judah, he left his servant there, while he himself went
a day's journey into the desert. He came to a broom tree, sat down
under it and prayed that he might die. "I have had enough, LORD,"
he said. "Take my life; I am no better than my ancestors."*

—1 Kings 19:1–4

What went wrong?

Angel Food Cake

A man who had been a U.S. pilot during World War II met a fellow who claimed that he had been a kamikaze pilot. "The war is all over now," he said. "Let's be friends. My name is Chow Mein."

"But kamikaze flyers were suicide pilots," said the American. "If you really had been one, you'd be dead now."

The former kamikaze pilot grinned and said, "I'm chicken Chow Mein."

Elijah turned chicken chow mein. Once He got Jezebel's message, he knew that his chicken was fricasseed. God's servant "was afraid and ran for his life [and] . . . came to Beersheba" (v. 3)—roughly one hundred fifty miles distant. That would wear anybody's emotional tread to a slick. Mind you, this was one hundred fifty miles on foot after a draining public ministry on Mt. Carmel (see 1 Kings 18:17–44), with a foot race against Ahab and his chariot sandwiched in between (see 1 Kings 18:45–46). And then Elijah ran, and ran, and ran until he staggered into Beersheba, only to outdo himself. He "left his servant there, while he himself went a day's journey into the desert. He came to a broom tree [and] sat down under it" (1 Kings 19:3–4). Then came the meltdown: "'I have had enough, LORD,' he said. 'Take my life; I am no better than my ancestors'" (v. 4).

And how did God respond?

"Why did you run like a coward, Elijah?"

"How could you defect when the people had just renounced Baal for Me?"

"Why did you embarrass heaven this way? Why did you embarrass Me this way?"

"Did you think I was deaf?"
"Did you think I was dumb?"
"Did you think I was blind?"
"Was my arthritis so bad, Elijah, that my arm could not save?"
No. No lectures. No sermons. Not even a fireside chat. It doesn't take a theologian to interpret what happened to the prophet. Elijah was one whipped pup. When his body quit, he quit.

But God still got His sermon in.

> *Then [Elijah] lay down under the tree and fell asleep. All at once an angel touched him and said, "Get up and eat." He looked around, and there by his head was a cake of bread baked over hot coals, and a jar of water. He ate and drank and then lay down again. The angel of the LORD came back a second time and touched him and said, "Get up and eat, for the journey is too much for you." So he got up and ate and drank.*
>
> —1 Kings 19:5–8

Some sleep. Some angel food cake. Bottled water. Some more sleep. Some more cake. God's wordless sermon. No matter how impressive Elijah's résumé was, the prophet was still clay.

We would be wise to remember that.

Rest

Researchers estimate that 50 to 85 percent of physical problems are stress-related. That includes everything from headaches to heart attacks. Stress—the disruption of normal bodily functions such as heart rate, blood pressure, and metabolism—places your body into a "fight or flight" mode. Long-term living in that mode lowers the body's ability to fight disease. Stress is like the tension on a violin string—to make music, there must be some, but too much stress can snap the string. Health experts say that if you wind up in a hospital bed, ask yourself, "Did my lifestyle put me here?" In more than 50 percent of the cases, the answer is yes.

Rest is not a sin. Relaxation is not a sin. Recreation is not a sin.

Sleep is not a sin. Naps are not a sin. Vacations are not a sin. Remember, the road to Beersheba is littered with good, ministry-committed, Elijah-type people whose schedule allows them no breathing room.

Exercise

Have you done any exercise today? Have you challenged your body to do more than blend with the decor? There's an old saying that football is twenty-two men down on the field in desperate need of rest, watched by eighty thousand people in the stands in desperate need of exercise.

But not any longer. We in North America are jogging, walking, swimming, and cycling our way into a healthier existence. People are rediscovering one of God's physiological laws—the body is designed to be used.

But a lot of energetic Christians snub that tenet. The belief still floats around that to serve Christ is to ignore such temporal matters. Did not Paul say, "For bodily discipline is only of little profit" (1 Tim. 4:8 NASB)?

He did. But the apostle didn't say that it's worthless. Remember, Paul's travels across the Roman Empire were not done in a Boeing 747. His legs did the walking. If he was not on a ship, Paul was on his feet. Doctors tell us over and over again, an exercise program—whether it's walking, running, or bicycling—reduces the risks of a multitude of diseases.

Have you done any exercises today?

Diet

Connections: salt and hypertension, cholesterol and heart disease, too much food and an expanding waistline. Fats, fats, fats. Sweets, sweets, sweets. Seconds. Maybe thirds. We all know that what we eat affects more than our taste buds.

You know that it is time for a diet when

- you dive into a swimming pool so your friends can go surfing;
- you have to apply your makeup with a paint roller;

- Weight Watchers demands your resignation;
- you step on a scale and it says, "One at a time, please";
- the bus driver asks you to sit on the other side because he wants to make a turn without flipping over;
- you're in the classroom at school and turn around and erase the entire blackboard;
- they throw puffed rice at your wedding;
- you hiccup wearing a bathing suit and you look like someone adjusting a venetian blind;
- you fall down and try to get up and rock yourself to sleep in the process; and
- a shipbuilder wants to use you as a model.

I wish I knew who made all these jokes so that credit isn't given to me. They sound so harsh. But sometimes it takes a harsh ring to get us to pick up the phone. Yes, some people who are heavy can't help it. No, they are not in the majority. And although I have no proof, it seems that a lot of Christians who campaign against alcohol abuse, tobacco abuse, and drug abuse are deaf and dumb when it comes to food abuse.

Pastor, are you in control of your intake? How about you, staff member? Para-church leader? If a fruit of the Spirit is self-control, maybe the table is the best place to find out how spiritual we really are.

None of these things—rest, exercise, and a healthy diet—makes one a super-Christian. But their lack can make for an ineffective one.

Katy really loves the Lord, and not just in word alone.[1] This dear lady, a middle-aged entrepreneur, never married and gives of herself as do few others in the body of Christ. In her ministry to others, Katy's pockets are deep. Missions. Children. Although she is successful, she will deny herself so that others might receive. What a blessing she is to the Lord's work and His people.

But if she gets more than four hours of sleep, Katy feels like a sluggard. Katy lives her business enterprise night and day. Competition is keen. Her exercise program? A computer keyboard—at least three hours each morning. Katy's diet? Not the smartest choices. She's diabetic and obese. A lethal combination. Doctors mince no words: "Madam, either shape up or you will get shipped out."

Katy is what Friedman and Rosenman call a Type A personality. The two cardiologists' comprehensive study related personality to cardiovascular disorders. After years of observations, interviews, and questionnaires, these doctors profiled the characteristics of stressed (Type A) and nonstressed (Type B) individuals. Two combined traits make up a Type A personality: an excessive competitive drive (beating out someone else) and a continual sense of urgency (a feeling of always having to meet deadlines). Type A's tend to be aggressive and extroverted, and they judge accomplishments in terms of numbers. Type A's cannot relax without guilt. Type B's, on the other hand, have just as much ambition as Type A's, but they are motivated by personal satisfaction rather than by competitiveness. Pressure will not affect a Type B's leisure. Doctors Rosenman and Friedman are convinced that Type A personalities are seven to ten times more likely to develop heart disease than are Type B personalities.

Katy is saved. Katy is a committed believer. Katy is also a walking time bomb—or was. She blew shortly after I wrote the preceding paragraphs.

No Better

An attractive young girl said to her friend, "Not only has Jeff broken my heart and wrecked my whole life but also he spoiled my entire evening!" That was how Elijah felt. Jezebel had not only shattered his whole life but also spoiled his entire evening. "I have had enough, LORD. . . . Take my life; I am no better than my ancestors" (1 Kings 19:4).

Such is the logic of a body that is uncared for. Under the broom tree, Elijah reasoned from false premises. Because he ignored the laws that God had built into his body, fatigue played with his mind, just as it does with ours.

The more we run, the more we tell ourselves, *I'm required. I'm necessary. Who else could marshal both fire and rain from heaven?* But our ecclesiastical scoreboard looks like that of most other ministers—a plateaued ministry, a declining ministry. Fatigue suckles the thought, *I'm really no better than others. I quit!*

The logic springing from a body that is uncared for leads to faulty conclusions.

Nat's fever began to rise on Sunday night. By Monday morning, it was out of sight—the sixth time in as many weeks. But his wife never called the doctor because Nat's fever is caused by what many pastors suffer on Monday mornings—resignation fever. In recent months, the statistics for Nat's church have not been what they once were. It is a church with great promise and probably the most gifted staff in the community, but the place has gone into a lull. Once everyone was so excited, so blessed—and they let others know about it. Now it's "so what"—and they let others know about that, too. Nat's racked his brains, put in extra hours, and sought out the latest church growth gurus. What is his conclusion? "I'm really no better than others. I ought to quit."

Sam teaches in a public school, but only because his teaching salary enables him to keep ministering to a small assembly of believers. An attendance of twenty-five would break all records. He is one of two elders, the Sunday school superintendent, song director, and janitor. On Saturday, he prepares for Sunday. Sunday after church, he prepares for Monday. By Tuesday, it's tough, especially if Sunday's attendance was low. And recently there's been a lot of low attendance on Sundays. His wife does not need a spiritual thermometer to know that Sam's got the fever. "I'm really no better than others. Somebody else could do this. Maybe I should quit."

The logic springing from a body that is uncared for drives us to do stupid things. Fatigue never reminds us that faithfulness, not nickels and noses, is what makes the headlines in heaven. Fatigue does not say, "Blaine, Nat, Sam, faithfulness in small things is a big thing to God." It never tells us that when nothing works, nothing but trust is what delights God. You will not hear fatigue say, "And without faith it is impossible to please Him, for he who comes to God must believe that He is, and that He is a rewarder of those who seek Him" (Heb. 11:6 NASB). It will not tell you that trusting God when God doesn't look like God is worship of His unseen perfection. Fatigue will tell you only to quit. The logic springing from a body that is uncared for always reasons away from God and His will.

Wake Up!

It nearly happened to me several times. Thankfully, I caught myself before it was too late. Lewis didn't catch himself. I heard it. The prayer group heard it. Before men and angels, Lewis let everyone know of his newfound rest in the Lord: while we prayed, he snored.

In times past, Lewis's prayers had been such an encouragement; when he interceded, we all sensed that heaven heard. If anyone had lingering doubts that Lewis was now asleep at the wheel, all of them had now been removed. The man snored so loudly that heaven couldn't help but hear. Once would have been enough, but it happened at the next three weekly prayer meetings. Just like clockwork. Ten minutes and he was out.

What an embarrassment! Not for Lewis—he never knew it—but for the rest of us. Because we did not do what needed to be done. After the first week some of us found out that Lewis's employer had increased his hours from forty to more than seventy hours a week. The man's body was a wreck. The most spiritual thing he could have done was stay home and go to bed. But none of us had the guts to wake him up and tell him.

Does someone need to wake you up? Do you care for your body?

> *Do you not know that your body is a temple of the Holy Spirit, who is in you, whom you have received from God? You are not your own; you were bought at a price. Therefore honor God with your body.*

—1 Corinthians 6:19

Isn't that the reason you don't shoot up heroin, snort cocaine, and bed down with prostitutes? Then it ought to be a good enough reason to get proper rest, sufficient exercise, and maintain a healthy diet.

It ought to be the reason you respect medical advice. In cases of diabetes, hypoglycemia, and other imbalances, for example, a doctor is necessary to ferret out the reason for fatigue. Don't think that it's unspiritual to listen to the medical establishment. Paul listened. Remember, he had a personal physician—Luke—with him to the very end (see 2 Tim. 4:6–11).

If your body is under stress, then more is going into your mental hopper than you probably suspect. Your decision-making process could very well be held hostage by your physical condition. Be alert to that possibility. Remember that the heart—with all of its facets—is the real you. The Spirit-controlled heart should dictate to the body, not vice versa. And if we keep the engine ahead of the caboose, we can make significant decisions—to go or to stay—in light of eternity, not in light of the weary here and now. Friend, it's always better to rest first and then act, than to act first and then regret.

9

SECOND THOUGHTS
Axioms of God's Will

From the minutes of a late-night meeting:
The motion is:
Whereas this place is no good for me and my family, I move that we leave.
Is there a second?
Yes.
All in favor let it be known by saying "Aye." Opposed?
It's unanimous; the motion passes. It's time to quit.

Who hasn't done that? In one of those late-night, mental business meetings, who hasn't questioned the goodness of a ministry setting? Something unexpected happens, and there's a motion on the table. Second thoughts second it. Following a lengthy debate, our emotions say "Aye." It's a done deal. Yes, we should move on.

Johnny Weissmuller, best known for his portrayal of Tarzan, was asked for the best advice he could give to a young actor. Weissmuller mused and then quipped, "Don't let go of the vine."[1]

That's good advice, especially when we're ready to say, "No more!" Not that a change in ministry or ministry locations is letting go of the vine. Believers who persevere can still pursue fresh opportunities. We follow a Lord who actively directs His own. From the big decisions down to the everyday choices, God's will is dynamic—lived out in an infinite number of settings, according to His unique plan for every individual. No. A change in ministry or ministry setting is not letting go of the vine.

A change of mind about God and His will is. Letting go of the vine is letting go of things that we once knew to be true. It's losing a grip on what we thought was heaven's design for us in the moral jungle of this world. With screams of "you will fail" and shrieks of "what might have been" coming from behind every tree and bush, we grow fatigued and conclude that

- this place is not good for me,
- this place is not good for my family, and
- this place does more harm than good.

Consider again Elijah. He, too, had gone into business session. On Mt. Carmel, reeling fire down from heaven, Elijah knew that God's will was the place to be. But when Queen Jezebel got word about the slaughter of her preachers and "faxed" Elijah: "May the gods deal with me, be it ever so severely, if by this time tomorrow I do not make your life like that of one of them" (1 Kings 19:2), second thoughts said, "Not so." For the prophet, God's will was the very last place he wanted to be, and he told God so. At the broom tree, Elijah

> . . . got up and ate and drank. Strengthened by that food, he traveled forty days and forty nights until he reached Horeb, the mountain of God. There he went into a cave and spent the night. And the word of the LORD came to him: "What are you doing here, Elijah?" He replied, "I have been very zealous for the LORD God Almighty. The Israelites have rejected your covenant, broken down your altars, and put your prophets to death with the sword. I am the only one left, and now they are trying to kill me too."
>
> —1 Kings 19:8–10

Elijah laid it out. Straightforward. No shame. The prophet brought heaven up to speed on the situation. He concluded that heaven had initiated a bad plan, and used lousy implementation, and now future prospects were horrible: "I am the only one left, and now they are trying to kill me, too" (v. 10). The will of God? Known, obeyed, shared—and it proved deficient.

Elijah let go of the vine.

NaCl

Guilty as charged—even before the first bite. No matter the meal, I'd reach for the shaker and douse my dinner in NaCl—sodium chloride, better known as salt. Tons of it.—like a blizzard on top of Mt. Everest. My wife, Debbie, prepared meals that were always a treat . . . if I had my salt. But my taste buds have become new creatures. No more snow-topped casseroles. No more powdered chicken breast. Debbie's entrees now satisfy on their own. No salt.

Have you ever salted God's plan for your life, seasoned it with your anticipations? "If I do God's will, my ministry will excel." Expectations of success—the salt of ministry.

Evidently, Elijah liked salt. He expected fire and rain on Mt. Carmel to produce revival in the streets. "Opposition? What opposition? They'll see that heaven does not back a flop!" God's will satisfied him as long as there was salt.

But somebody forgot the shaker. Feel Elijah's keen disappointment when he later groaned:

I have been very zealous for the LORD God Almighty.

—(v. 10)

"For three years, I've stuck my neck out . . . gave it my best. And what do I have to show for it? Blistered feet and a queen who does not know how to lose with grace!"

Where's the salt?

The sense of accomplishment?

Enjoyment?

The blessings?

Success?

All went so well—fire, repentant people, rain. Then one woman said, "No." From that moment on, God's will for Elijah ceased to elate.

Could the same be said of you? Can you look at some incident in your past as the moment when God's will ceased to satisfy you? You once were happy, at rest within, relishing the highest of hopes. But no more. The salt—it's just not there. Outcome? You now push away what heaven's cooked up for you.

Becky Moser's name is a household word—in heaven. Along with her husband, Ed, she worked among the Seri Indians on the Baja Peninsula of western Mexico as a Wycliffe Bible Translator. For twenty-five years, Becky and Ed worked as a team in a village of one hundred fifty people. Then Ed died just as the first draft of the New Testament had been completed. But much still needed to be done to get the Word into the hands of the Seri. Becky did it. It was especially hard sitting down at her husband's desk and sorting through the unfinished manuscripts. But she did it and finished within six years of Ed's home-going.

And the Seri Indians? Bernie May, former Wycliffe director, says,

> The people don't seem to care very much. As I walked through the village I thought of that verse in John: "And the light shineth in darkness, and the darkness comprehended it not." That made no difference to Becky. Her task was to fulfill the Great Commission of her Lord—to take the Word to a lost world. Becky took me into her hut and showed me her prized possession. It was a big jar of alcohol—full of what she called "belly buttons."
>
> Some years ago a Seri woman was having trouble in childbirth. Becky acted as midwife and saved the child's life. Several weeks later this woman came to Becky's hut with the baby's umbilical cord in a jar of alcohol. It was her way of expressing her thanks for saving the baby's life, since a Seri child's umbilical cord is considered a family treasure. Over the years Becky has saved the lives of other children. Now she has a jar full of "belly buttons"—more than twenty—each one representing a child. That's all Becky Moser has to show for the thirty-one years of work among the Seri Indians. A jar full of belly buttons and a finished New Testament.

There's no thriving church. Not even much interest among the people except for a few families who have become Christians. Not much to show for all those years of work . . . [yet] somehow she thinks her Bibles and belly buttons are sufficient.[2]

Is God's will flat, less than satisfying? Jesus says, "My food . . . is to do the will of him who sent me and to finish his work" (John 4:34). Our Lord speaks as one supremely satisfied with the will of the Father.

So what gives with us when all we have is a jar full of "belly buttons" and, unlike Becky Moser, it is not sufficient? If the problem is not with the spiritual food, where is it? It's our taste buds, our desensitized taste buds—affected as they are by our bottom-line culture and our failure to adjust to a divine plan that God dishes out, but chooses not to salt.

When God chooses not to season with the salt of our expectations, there's not a lot we can do about it except learn to appreciate God's food the way He serves it. It's a fundamental truth—God's will is capable of satisfying in and of itself regardless of whether we enjoy the seasoning of our expectations or not. Yet, when we want to quit, it's a truth about God's will that we let go of.

Have you collected a lot of belly buttons lately? Is that what bothers you? Then don't leave until it doesn't. Learn to take your ministry plain, like Becky Moser took hers—without salt. Taste buds addicted to success, as the world measures success, puts you in spiritual danger, and God knows it. Just as too much salt is bad for the body, too much of the worldly kind of success can be bad for the soul. The believer who's only happy with his or her salt is an NaCl addict. If you feel ecstatic over the successes but whipped by their absence, then God's food for you—His will—does not satisfy. You minister for the extras. To make a move before God has weaned you could mean never seeing the salt shaker again.

That's not to say that God doesn't dispense salt. God wants us to want to bear fruit, and that includes the kind of fruit that we and others can see, maybe even what the world would call success. But salt is not necessary to bear fruit from His will. God's will, with or without the salt of our expectations, satisfies in and of itself. That's a truth we dare not let go of when considering if it's time to quit.

Discerning the Difference

You might well ask, "Does that mean that every time I feel restless within it's because I am not satisfied with God's will? Isn't it possible that a lack of peace might be an indicator that it's God's will for me to move on?"

Indeed it could. Paul himself considered lack of peace to be a guiding principle when discerning God's will. Paul wrote to the Corinthians,

> *Now when I went to Troas to preach the gospel of Christ and found that the Lord had opened a door for me, I still had no peace of mind, because I did not find my brother Titus there. So I said good-by to them and went on to Macedonia.*
>
> —2 Corinthians 2:12–13

No peace of mind. Amazing! The apostle had a wide open door for the gospel but refused to go through it. He lacked the inner confirmation.

So how do you differentiate between the restlessness that is a signal from above and the restlessness that is not?

People whom you and I respect err at this very point. After ten years in the land of Canaan waiting for a child, Abraham and Sarah decided that something had to be done. To them, no peace over no junior translated into "Heaven says make a move." The result? Hagar, a young slave girl, became pregnant with a child that was never accepted (see Gen. 16:3–6). More than two thousand years later, Simon Peter was definitely not at peace with the turn of events. Provoked over what others did to his Lord, he swung his weapon. Chop! He missed, getting just an ear, and he discovered how far off the mark he really was when Jesus said, "Put your sword away! Shall I not drink the cup the Father has given me?" (John 18:11). Believers often mistake a lack of peace within for God's seconding of their motions to implement new ideas. And they live to regret it.

So how do you tell the difference? Take a few days away from the situation—if that's possible—and biblically sort through things.

- Are you willing to forego any future ministry for the sake of the people to whom you minister now? Moses told the Lord, "Blot me out of the book you have written" (Exod. 32:32) if God would not forgive the congregation and continue to call Israel His own.
- Do you, like Paul, grieve over those to whom you minister? He wrote, "I speak the truth in Christ—I am not lying, my conscience confirms it in the Holy Spirit—I have great sorrow and unceasing anguish in my heart. For I could wish that I myself were cursed and cut off from Christ for the sake of my brothers, those of my own race, the people of Israel" (Rom. 9:1–4).
- If this is the ministry ground where God wants you to "fall in," would you? Jesus said, "I tell you the truth, unless a kernel of wheat falls to the ground and dies, it remains only a single seed. But if it dies, it produces many seeds. The man who loves his life will lose it, while the man who hates his life in this world will keep it for eternal life. Whoever serves me must follow me; and where I am, my servant also will be. My Father will honor the one who serves me" (John 12:24–26).

James tells us, "Come near to God and he will come near to you" (James 4:8). Get away with the Word, a pencil and pad, and then pray, even fast. In the presence of the Lord, an honest search always yields honest results. The inner restlessness might be God. It might be a hankering after salt. Take some time away, and ask the hard questions. Write down the answers. Find out.

Father Knows Best

Elijah answered his own questions. He did more than just assume that God's will should always result in outward signs of success. He questioned its preeminence. Was it really best? In fact, by the time Elijah arrived at Horeb, the mountain of God, he had concluded that if God's will was best, then He must make it so. Notice again Elijah's lament: "I have been very zealous for the LORD God Almighty. The Israelites have rejected your covenant, broken down your altars, and put your prophets to death with the sword. I am the only one left" (1 Kings 19:10).

That was not best—at least the prophet didn't think so. No one could convince Elijah that it was best to be the only prophet in Israel. Things shouldn't have deteriorated to that state. For God's will to be best, adjustments should have been made.

But what adjustments? How does one make God's will best? We cannot. There is no way to make it so. As one does not make water wet or the sky blue, neither do we make God's will best. It just is. When Paul states in Romans 12:2 that our Lord's will is "good, pleasing and perfect," the apostle doesn't qualify his claim with footnotes. His statement, like a blanket, covers all. Happy ministries. Grief-filled ministries. Increasing ministries. Decreasing ministries. If God is good, His will is good. If God is pleasing, His will is pleasing. If God is perfect, His will is perfect. It is impossible for it to be otherwise— without God's being otherwise.

That means that it was indeed best for Elijah to stand alone against the forces of evil, even if he was the last survivor at Israel's version of the Alamo—which, by the way, he was not (see 1 Kings 19:18). No matter where Elijah found himself—assuming that he was not in willful sin—God's plan for him to be there was good, pleasing, and perfect because his God was good, pleasing, and perfect.

Did you say that your present situation is not best? Just remember that *best* is defined for the believer not in terms of ideal settings—nice house, nice neighborhood, nice family, nice job, nice church, nice ministry, nice whatever—but in terms of God and who He is. If He chose a particular setting for you that is not nice, it does not mean that it's not best. What makes it best is His use of it. His goodness guarantees nothing but the greatest possible good for us in the light of eternity. His pleasure includes pleasurable goals accomplished through His use of the situation, pleasurable not only to Him but also someday to us. God's perfection makes His use of it absolutely perfect, just what we need. Thus, a given situation does not stop being best until

God makes clear that He no longer chooses to use it. Remember, *best* is defined in terms of God's choices and who He is.

God's will as we live it out is also best for our loved ones and friends. For example, when God chose not to deal with Jezebel until some years later (see 1 Kings 21:23; 2 Kings 9:30–37), that plan was good, pleasing, and perfect not only for Elijah but also for the prophet's servant. Don't forget him. He was the one who fled with Elijah, never dreaming that in the shuffle he would get dumped off in Beersheba (see 1 Kings 19:3–4)—closer to Jezebel's reach than was Elijah! Granted, to the queen his blood wasn't Elijah's blood, but it was still red. Some butchers aren't picky.

Remember, God's will for one believer at times has implications for others, which makes it God's will for *each person* involved. And because heaven's plan is always best, it is best for those dear ones, too.

So you want to leave your current ministry, maybe the ministry itself? Are others involved? Then ensure that you don't use them as an excuse for your actions. In God's sight, what is good for one is good for all.

Ron and Mary had a problem. The church that Ron shepherded was putting on the pressure, primarily because the two were not like the former pastor and his wife. It was nothing to hear, "Pastor Jerry and his family never did that!" And, as is sometimes the case, the one who had the toughest time with criticism was the lady. Ron had the hide of a rhinoceros; Mary the skin of a babe. He could stick it out; she wanted nothing but out. They wondered if they should resign and find some other form of financial support, at least for a while.

Mary was convinced that it was best for her but unsure if it would be for Ron. Ron thought that it was best to stay, but he was unsure if it was best for Mary. Mary could have demanded that they go—"If you love me, you'll leave"—but what would that have done to Ron and his ministry? Churches these days do not cotton to has-beens. Ron could have stayed, and he wanted to, but what would it have done to his wife. Push her over the edge? It was a mess.

But no more. The church did not make a decision to adjust. Ron and Mary did. The two accepted the proposition that because God's will is best, it is best for both of them. For Ron, that meant that God might use his wife's difficulty to direct him into a leave of absence from vocational ministry. If so, it would be best for both her and him. Or it could be that God wanted Mary to persevere and learn of the sufficiency of divine grace in the midst of criticism. Again, if that was the case, it would be best for both him and her. The focus was no longer Ron and Mary; the focus finally became God. They knew that His will for one of them was His will for both of them. And it would be best.

By the way, they stayed.

We might not feel it, and we might have trouble believing it, but based on who God is and what He does, God's will is always best—for all who may be involved. Of course, that takes faith—nothing less. Faith knows that time will prove God's will to be best. When? Faith does not know exactly, but that doesn't matter. Faith sees the unseen and is content to wait.

Unbelief is discontented. It tries to explain the unexplainable but cannot. The conclusion? It must not be best. Therefore, unbelief quits with barely a second thought.

Faith simply cannot do that. Sure it's hard. No, faith cannot explain the unexplainable. And indeed present circumstances might not look the best—for anybody. But faith does not look at *now* for what is best; it looks to God—and finds the best. For faith realizes that He is good, pleasing, and perfect; thus, so is His will.

If you are contemplating a change, don't let go of the truth—God's will is always best. If you do, from then on *best* must be defined in terms of something less than Him. And that's ominous.

Safe

It was my oldest daughter's first picture dressed as a little lady. Wearing a deep-green velvet vest, beige blouse, and plaid skirt, Carrie Anne charmed even the most casual observer. Her other pictures were baby-like; this one captured embryonic adulthood. And I murdered it.

Not intentionally. But that doesn't matter. The portrait is marred for good. One day, while cleaning marks off the ceiling, my elbow knocked the cleanser off the ladder, and it spilled all over the portrait.

Long drips ran down the face and onto the vest, blouse, and skirt. Yellow streaks. Lots of them.

Sick is not the word. My face was funeral pale. The gift of my daughter's youth entrusted to my safe-keeping—and I wrecked it. How could I have been so stupid? If I had just moved the picture.

Elijah's response to the Lord's inquiry at Mt. Horeb—"What are you doing here?"— reveals another problem the prophet had with God's will: it's not always a safe place to be. The prophet implied that, like a careless father, God had spilled needless pain all over his life. "I have been very zealous for the LORD God Almighty. The Israelites have rejected your covenant, broken down your altars, and put your prophets to death with the sword. I am the only one left, *and now they are trying to kill me too*" (1 Kings 19:10, italics added). A beautiful portrait: fervor for God, a passion, a zeal embryonic of things to come . . . and now this mess spilled all over it. What a way to wreck a life! If God had just moved the picture.

Is God's will safe?

Before Jezebel's threat, the prophet would have boomed, "Without question!" Because of that conviction, Elijah had stood for God as one against thousands on Mt. Carmel. He put his own hide right on the line, convinced that the safest place for any individual was the will of God. But then Jezebel went ballistic. Now, for Elijah, that same divine will was the riskiest place to be.

Just as believers confess that God's will satisfies and is best, Christians also hold to the truth that God's will is safe—until something or someone blows. Then we usually do what Elijah did—grab up those things that are dear to us and run. Elijah's "thing" was his life. For us it could be happiness, security, respectability—you fill in the blank. Once we suspect that God is snoozing, you and I make a grab for control. If heaven won't take care of what's dear to us, who will?

Answer? Nobody. To think otherwise is myopic. What is ours now is just that—for now. We hold such treasures only between the crib and the crypt. Come that last breath, we'll have to let go. No earthling can take care— in the absolute sense—of anything.

So what should we do? Either lose what we hold dear for good or give it to the One who is not bound by time. Paul writes, "I know whom I have believed, and am convinced that he is able to guard what I have entrusted to Him for that day" (2 Tim. 1:12). For what day? That day dated beyond His and our death certificates. God always takes care of that which has been deposited with Him. And that is just as true for your "self" as it is for the other things you cherish. Paul also wrote, "The Lord will rescue me from every evil attack and will bring me safely to his heavenly kingdom. To him be glory for ever and ever. Amen" (2 Tim. 4:18). You will make it home intact, with all those other *things* cared for to your complete eternal delight.

To give all to God, though, does not mean that you will never ache. Obedience in this matter is not an insurance policy against tragedy. Pain is still our portion on this earth. Yet, eternity will be an everlasting testimony to the fact that God's will was, is, and will be forever safe.

Great-Grandfather Time

The following is a letter that my youngest daughter wrote as an assignment in the third grade:

November 1995

Dear Grandchild,

The time has come for you to learn about the past. I was 8 years old in 1995. We had to use wooden sticks to write with. I was in Mrs. Jackson's class. Our class probably isn't as big as yours. We had a big black thing on the wall. If Mrs. Jackson had work for the whole class to do, she would write it on the black thing. And can you believe it? We had to write on wooden things called desks.

We were taught fancy handwriting called "cursive." Here's my name in "cursive":

Amy Michelle Allen

I also knew something called "calligraphy." Here's my name in "calligraphy":

Amy Michelle Allen

If a book fair was at school, we got a slip of paper. (It told that we were having one.)

Love, your Grandmother

When my Amy brought it home, I thought, "Cute letter, really cute. What a neat assignment!" . . . until it dawned on me . . . if Amy was a grandmother, that made yours truly a great-grandfather, who's maybe in a wheelchair, gumming his food, or perhaps even checked out, for good. Wow! That's a jolt! Great-grandfather time. By then, with one foot in the grave and the other on a banana peel, decisions made are decisions that can never be undone. Within the context of God's grace, what's done is lived with forever.

And, servant of Christ, so it is for you. The decisions you make now, come banana-peel time, are decisions you live with forever. Neither you nor I want 20/20 hindsight that sees only regret.

That's the reason for this chapter. There's nothing new. Everything in it is simply a reminder. You've been taught in various ways that God's will satisfies, is best, and is the safest place to be. You've been taught this and have probably even taught it yourself. But because we are of the same nature as Elijah (see James 5:17)—chicken—there is not a believer who, when threatened, hasn't second-guessed God's will. Just make certain that quitting now—whatever that might involve for you—is not letting go of heaven's plan for your life. To act because you are suddenly persuaded that God's will is no longer true satisfaction, the absolute best, and infinitely secure is to set yourself up for some pretty unpleasant great-grandfather time.

Only you and God know why you want to quit. If you make your move because of a change in the way you view God's will, you certainly won't be the first. If misery loves company, you'll have both. Others, like the prophets, have gone before you. A lot of others.

But misery wants something else besides company; misery seeks relief. And that's something that you won't find by skipping out on God. Rationalizing with the most spiritual-sounding logic will not change eternal facts about God's will. What Jesus said two thousand years ago is still good today:

> *"Take my yoke upon you and learn from me, for I am gentle and humble in heart, and you will find rest for your souls. For my yoke is easy and my burden is light."*
>
> —Matthew 11:29–30

10

COST AUDIT
When God Says "Do" and You Don't

"CONTENTMENT IS A NATURAL wealth; luxury, artificial poverty." So said Greek philosopher Socrates. Contentment is an inner quietness irrespective of attending accoutrements. More than any other people, kingdom children should know that. Because of God's grace, no matter what the surroundings, contentment is our true wealth.

Remember Moses? Elijah? Each knew of the adequacy of God, but at least once in their lives, the grave rather than grace enticed them more. What one knows is not always what one practices.

Add Jonah to that elite group. You remember him, don't you? He's the one who discovered something fishy about God's plan for his life. Like Moses and Elijah, this prophet opted for early retirement, but with a difference. His calling it quits was not a one-time occurrence. In fact, Jonah is indelibly marked by sacred history as a quitter. Other than 2 Kings 14:25 and the book that bears his name, no other Old Testament reference to the prophet exists, and even his book is a four-chapter account punctuated with failure.

Why such a distinguished label? Jonah had his reasons—some of them even match Moses' and Elijah's rationalizations. But just as there are no cloned snowflakes, so there are no identical motives. Each person's decisions reflect his or her own pattern of considerations.

Jonah's reasons? The accoutrements. He did not have peace being where God wanted him. The mission field—both the people and the appointments—were not to his liking. And he told heaven about it. He told pagans. His family and friends found out. Even you and I know about it. From day one, Jonah hated God's plan with a passion. And it cost him.

How much? We may never know. But the numbers on the price tag indicate that it's more than we would want to pay. Jonah almost bought the farm. Or should we say the aquarium?

Forget It

Go to Nineveh.
Preach against it.
One verse but two imperatives, both issued by God. He wanted a job done. Pronto.

> *"Go to the great city of Nineveh and preach against it, because its wickedness has come up before me."*
>
> —Jonah 1:2

Could heaven be any more articulate? We sometimes might wonder what God's will is in a given situation. Not Jonah. He knew. No doubts. No need for godly counsel. No reason for prayer and fasting.

And how did he respond?

"Forget it."

Rebellion of the worst sort. It's one thing to disobey the Lord when things begin to sour. That sort of disobedience results from no longer believing that God rules from His throne. It's quite another matter, however, to rebel because we don't *want* to do what we've been told to do. That's premeditated disobedience—our wills against God's will—long before things go wrong. Both kinds of disobedience are inexcusable, but the latter kind is more odious.

Which brings us back to you and me. In wanting to quit, have we done like Jonah? Have we told God, "Thanks, but no thanks—this is not what I had in mind"? That Jonah's story is a part of the Bible is evidence that God expected some of His own children to do just that. Kingdom children have kissed off God—and sometimes still do.

But they need to know the consequences. And that's why we have the book of Jonah. Scripture says that for the believer, "There is now no condemnation for those who are in Christ Jesus" (Rom. 8:1). It doesn't say, "There are now no *consequences* for those who are in Christ Jesus." Anarchy against God sets off a chain reaction. Strutting away from what you and I know to be God's will carries a price tag.

Before you quit, have you done a disobedience cost audit? Is quitting your current ministry a message to God—"Stick it in your ear"? If so, it's a green light to Him: "God, now You stick it to me." Too many people have sighed *if only I could do it over* for us to think that rebellion is immune from God's discipline. It is not. Once a believer sets his face like flint to go against God's revealed will, spiritual laws come into play.

Then it's the domino effect.

It happened to Jonah. It could happen to you and me.

Smooth Sailing

Have you ever been deep-sea fishing? I have—once. Just before the break of dawn, six of us sailed about thirty miles out into the Atlantic off the northeastern coast of Florida. The sunrise was unexcelled—fiery orange, passionate pink, a velvet blue.

So they told me. I didn't see it. I didn't want to see it. I was in the cabin below. The whitecaps were too much. No sooner had we sailed beyond the mouth of the river and into the Atlantic than I turned green around the gills. I mean really green. Ten minutes. That's all it took. A full day outing before me, and within ten minutes I had lost it all. Up front, I knew that I was where I ought not to be.

For Jonah, the first moments outside the will of God cost him nothing. He had no reason to think that he was where he ought not to be.

> *But Jonah ran away from the LORD and headed for Tarshish. He went down to Joppa, where he found a ship bound for that port. After paying the fare, he went aboard and sailed for Tarshish to flee from the LORD.*
> —Jonah 1:3

Things were working out great!

A ship in port.
Destination 180 degrees from Nineveh.
Space available.
Fare within budget.
Many moons away from Nineveh.
And best of all, the ship was ready to set sail.

Bon voyage! A travel agent could not have planned it better. This was a Mediterranean cruise with even the whitecaps a godsend—back and forth, back and forth, back and forth—until "Jonah had gone below deck, where he lay down and fell into a deep sleep" (v. 5).

The lesson? Satan knows that nobody wants unpleasant surprises. Smooth sailing is more to our liking. That's why Satan, as your travel agent, is more than glad to plan an itinerary with as little unpleasantness as possible. When we say, "Sorry, God," Satan wants to ensure that our departure is without regret.

Don't underestimate the first consequence of disobedience: all will probably go your way. So much so that your decision might even begin to look right.

Ship in port.
Destination the opposite direction.
Fare within your budget.
And it leaves now.

What more confirmation is needed that this is the right decision? You like what you see. You enjoy what you feel. You take pleasure in what you hear. God's will? Why think about that now? You're gone. Nothing discourages you. Absolutely nothing. You're not even seasick. Just smooth sailing. Besides, the more you think about it, the more it even looks like God's will!

"So Blaine," you ask, "if the factors in favor of making a change 'line up,' then I know it's not God?"

Of course not. When God leads us into a new sphere, the pieces of the puzzle will usually come together. But we need to be sure who's arranging the pieces. The answer depends on the value we place on the Lord's presence. Is it important to us? That was something to which Jonah hadn't given much thought. A boat. A cruise. An escape from what he didn't want to do. Jonah didn't give a second thought to what he pursued, if it would enhance or strain his friendship with the Lord.

I taught algebra between undergraduate and graduate school. One particular day was not to be an ordinary school day. Into my classroom walked the wife of the vice president of the United States. She was campaigning for her husband, who was in the run for the White House. While in our city she needed to be seen in an urban public school. So there she was—right in my classroom, cameras and all. And there I was—in front of thirty students with no doubt about who was the greatest among us all.

But that was mere mortals in the presence of another mere mortal. How much greater to be in the presence of deity! God is more important than any person or place. He overshadows everything. The psalmist said, "But as for me, it is good to be near God" (Ps. 73:28). Followers of Christ may at times lack a sense of God's nearness. We never lack His presence, but we sometimes lack the *awareness* of His presence. But we cannot stay like that for long. True believers long to be close to their God. He—not locations, attending circumstances, or people— is their *good*. God makes the ordinary a place where there's no doubt about who's the greatest among all.

So it's a fair question: When things line up in favor of changing to a new place, will God be your *good* there? Is that why you want to go? Is it a place where you can thoroughly enjoy His presence? Or do you, like Jonah, say, "Who cares?"

Have you ever been around a person whom you weren't excited about being around? Maybe it was a coworker, a blind date, or someone else with whom you didn't see eye-to-eye? Although both you and the other person might be in the same room, you're not on the same wavelength. The conversations are at best stilted. Then someone walks in with whom you are in sync, and the conversation changes—and how! You and the walk-in share not only the room but also your hearts. You listen carefully to each other. You give of yourselves. You are both alert to and revel in a cherished presence.

We always share the same room with God. He is omnipresent—in all places at all times:

> *Where can I go from your Spirit?*
>   *Where can I flee from your presence?*
> *If I go up to the heavens, you are there;*
>   *if I make my bed in the depths, you are there.*
> *If I rise on the wings of the dawn,*
>   *if I settle on the far side of the sea,*
> *even there your hand will guide me,*
>   *your right hand will hold me fast.*
>
> —Psalm 139:7–10

But being in the same room with God does not necessarily mean enjoying His company. Conversations with Him—prayer—are at best, stilted. His conversations with us—the Word . . . well, "Has the paper arrived yet?" Talking, but not sharing. Hearing, but not listening. Is that where you are now?

If so, and if you have an attractive opportunity to move, then without question the situation is suspect. If the opportunity would not enhance your fellowship with the Lord, the alarm bells should be deafening. Okay, so you're not as bad as Jonah. He fled from the presence of the Lord. But if you are in pursuit of the suspicious, is there much difference?

God's Response

Have you ever misplaced an address? The dresser? No, it's not there. My pocket? No, not there. Maybe I put it in my wallet? "Dear, have you seen my wallet?" Omniscience must be nice.

> *Then the LORD sent a great wind on the sea, and such a violent storm arose that the ship threatened to break up.*
>
> —Jonah 1:4

Jonah's Carnival cruise was over. God's response was decisive and forceful. How will it come to us? When? Where? We don't know, but it will come. If you are His child and choose to board the next ship out of Joppa, count on it. We might misplace an address, but God doesn't. He has yet to lose track of anyone, especially a Jonah.

"But how can a God of love do something like that?"

No. The question is How can He *not* do it? Love gives Him no choice. For that matter neither does His holiness, wisdom, immutability, sovereignty, omniscience, omnipresence, or omnipotence give Him a choice. Everything that God is screams for a response when His child chooses to hit the road. God would cease to be God if He let one of His own disobey without His intervention.

It might first come as inner nudges from the Spirit: "This is not right." The intensity may then increase—more overt actions—roadblocks along the way. He might even bring death. But mark it down: heaven *will* act. The response will be decisive and forceful.

That's sobering. There's no way to dress it up. We put ourselves on the wrong end of the rod of discipline when we tell God, "I've got other plans." We're asking to get clobbered—in love, true—but clobbered nonetheless.

It's Getting Dark

A soldier marching in parade formation waved to one of the spectators. The drill instructor darted over to the young man and growled, "Soldier, don't ever do that again!" But as his company marched past the reviewing stand, the young man waved a second time. When the troops got back to the barracks, the drill instructor barreled in and barked at the soldier, "I told you not to wave! Aren't you afraid of me?"

"Yes, sir," the private replied, "but you don't know my mother!"[1]

Jonah, before "the Reviewing Stand," didn't flinch, much less wave. Out in the Mediterranean in the middle of the mother of all squalls, the runaway prophet was as lifeless to what was going on around him as a patient in surgery. The Hebrew word translated *sleep* describes a deep, heavy sedation. Jonah was out! And not just physically; morally the man had gone numb. Scripture says that once the storm struck,

> All the sailors were afraid and each cried out to his own god. And they threw the cargo into the sea to lighten the ship. But Jonah had gone below deck, where he lay down and fell into a deep sleep. The captain

went to him and said, "How can you sleep? Get up and call on your
god! Maybe he will take notice of us, and we will not perish."

—Jonah 1:5–6

What an indictment! Jonah didn't give a rip what his disobedience did to others. He sacked out without a second thought for a boatload of lost men who were moments from eternity. Only after a pagan called him to prayer did Jonah digest the implications of his iniquity. On the inside, Jonah had turned to stone.

The greatest loss that the prophet suffered in quitting on God was not his reputation. His greatest loss was his heart. Jonah had gone from a state of usefulness—evidenced by God's wanting to entrust a critical ministry to him—to a state of *rock*.

That's a warning to every believer. You and I have nothing greater to lose than our hearts. No wonder Scripture exhorts, "Above all else, guard your heart, for it is the wellspring of life" (Prov. 4:23). To the Lord, nothing is more crucial to His use of us. "The LORD does not look at the things man looks at. Man looks at the outward appearance, but the LORD looks at the heart" (1 Sam. 16:7). If you lose anything, don't lose your heart.

Jonah did. His heart petrified in no time, starting with his first *no*. By rejecting light—God's revealed will for his life—Jonah lost more light. A heart that once was tender toward both God and men soon wanted absolutely nothing to do with either.

An American Christmas without lights on the tree would be like an American hamburger without meat on the bun. The two go together—or at least in the Allen family. And when it comes to Christmas lights, I am the one who is responsible for getting them on the tree and burning. In the early years, I checked each bulb before I strung them on the tree. If one bulb on a string of lights burned out, none of the others would shine. Either all worked or none worked. If I decorated a Christmas tree without knowing that a bulb was burned out, I had to search light by light, pawing through balls, branches, and bows to find the culprit.

But that, of course, was long before the Flood. Now I buy the other kind of lights—strings that will continue to shine even if a bulb burns out. When one goes, I know immediately where to put the replacement. But on the box is the following warning:

> Replace burned-out bulbs immediately. Nonreplaced burned-out bulbs cause remaining lit bulbs to burn out prematurely.

The manufacturer tells the truth. I can bear witness to that warning. One dead bulb, and the others drop like flies.

Jonah could bear witness, too. God gave him his light: "Go to the great city of Nineveh and preach against it, because its wickedness has come up before me" (1:2). And Jonah rejected it. But rather than quickly replace the burned-out bulb by repenting, he decided to live with it. The result? Jonah lost other lights, too, including

- prayer,
- compassion,
- responsibility,
- righteousness, and
- worship.

It all happened so fast. The bulbs didn't even flicker. They just went dead. Soon Jonah was a man in darkness. His own darkness. And he was comfortable with it! God had given light, and Jonah had rejected that light. It nearly cost him everything.

And, friend, it will cost us, too. If we take a direction that's not the light God has given to us, if we don't attend to that first burned-out bulb, we'll lose our whole string of lights. It'll get dark. Not all at once. Just bulb by bulb—so to seem nonthreatening. A nonthreatening darkness becomes comfortable. It becomes a darkness that will cover deeds we on brighter days never would have embraced. It happened to Jonah. It's happened to others. It'll happen to us.

> Replace burned-out bulbs immediately. Nonreplaced burned-out bulbs cause remaining lit bulbs to burn out prematurely.

Accountability

Time ran out for Jonah. It always does for a runaway child of God.

> *Then the sailors said to each other, "Come, let us cast lots to find*
> *out who is responsible for this calamity." They cast lots and the lot*
> *fell on Jonah. So they asked him, "Tell us, who is responsible for*
> *making all this trouble for us? What do you do? Where do you*
> *come from? What is your country? From what people are you?"*
>
> —Jonah 1:7–8

A sad day, indeed. God's prophet was caught. And by, of all people, pagans. Now his dirty linen would be hung out for all to see.

> *He answered, "I am a Hebrew and I worship the LORD, the God*
> *of heaven, who made the sea and the land." This terrified them and*
> *they asked, "What have you done?" (They knew he was running*
> *away from the LORD because he had already told them so.)*
>
> —Jonah 1:9–10

Found out in his shame? Yes, but there's more. The Bible reveals that the sailors tried everything in the book to save Jonah's hide. But nothing worked—nothing except what the prophet knew would right the wrong:

> *Then they took Jonah and threw him overboard, and the raging sea*
> *grew calm. . . . But the LORD provided a great fish to swallow*
> *Jonah, and Jonah was inside the fish three days and three nights.*
>
> —Jonah 1:15, 17

"Blaine," you say, "getting swallowed by a whale would never happen to me."

Don't be so certain. Sure, you won't eyeball a great fish. But don't forget, God has more than fins in His aquarium.

"But for me to quit now would not be as flagrant an act of disobedience as Jonah's. Big disobedience, big discipline. Little disobedience, little discipline."

Again, don't be so sure. Those pagan sailors on ship with Jonah were most likely Phoenicians, a people who were rooted in Canaanite religion. They bowed to a smorgasbord of deities—deities that were a thin disguise for Satan and his demons—and were given over to sex, licentiousness, barbarity, you name it. Jonah never behaved like that. Yet, who ended up overboard? God didn't touch the pagan sailors, but Jonah took a bath—a clue that accountability is not based on behavior alone.

Jesus said of those who opposed Him,

> *"If I had not come and spoken to them, they would not be guilty of sin. Now, however, they have no excuse for their sin. . . . If I had not done among them what no one else did, they would not be guilty of sin. But now they have seen these miracles, and yet they have hated both me and my Father."*
>
> —John 15:22, 24

The implication? It's hard to dodge. When it comes to accountability, behavior alone is not the basis for God's response. God also looks at what we ought to know. Certain things become our sin that would not be our sin if the light of truth had not been shone on those areas. Truth revealed adjudicates punishment received. Before you quit, take inventory on the light that God has shared with you—not with your ministerial peer, your seminary buddy, or your spouse—but with you.

> *So then* each one of us *shall give account of himself to God.*
>
> —Romans 14:12 NASB, emphasis added

Queasy?

We don't like to think about such things. They menace our impressions of God. As long as He acts as He is supposed to act, we are comfy. But to toss us overboard?

Yes, He will toss a Jonah overboard. If you are His child and willfully walk away from a place, a ministry, a life where He wants you to stay, you might get more than your piggies wet.

Love compels Him. Wisdom compels Him. Knowledge, faithfulness, and sovereignty compel Him. He's decreed that, as His child, you will never suffer the fate of others: "But when we are judged, we are disciplined by the Lord in order that we may not be condemned along with the world" (1 Cor. 11:32 NASB). Thrown overboard so that you won't suffer the same fate as the world—condemnation. It's certain that we'll get wet if we go where God says, "Don't." Romans 8:1 says, "Therefore, there is now no condemnation for those who are in Christ Jesus." God guarantees it with disciplinary action.

So if you take a walk, and it's not with God's blessing, it might be on the plank.

Don't.

11

THUMBS
Praise and Packing Your Bags

THEY WERE AT IT AGAIN—Hillary, Brandy, and our daughter Carrie Anne. This time it was over a caterpillar. That's right. A caterpillar had made the worst decision in its life: it had traversed the sandbox where the three kids played house.

"It's mine!" Brandy shrieked.

"No, it's mine!" Hillary bristled. And the two were on the mat.

Carrie Anne, the ref among the three, knew that something had to be done. Among all of her friends, Hillary had the coldest blood. What she could not have, she made sure no one else could have—caterpillars being no exception. Carrie Anne jumped in and thundered, "You're both wrong. That caterpillar belongs to God!"

Isn't it nice when someone has a definitive word? Especially when it's a word from God. It's good to know that someone—raising the spiritual decibel level in our ears—has a sure word from Him.

Jonah had just that. Once he got his act together, he arrived in Nineveh to deliver God's message: "Yet forty days and Nineveh will be overthrown" (Jonah 3:4 NASB). In the Hebrew text, that phrase accounts for just five words—short and not so sweet.

The impact?

> *The Ninevites believed God. They declared a fast, and all of them, from the greatest to the least, put on sackcloth. When the news*

reached the king of Nineveh, he rose from his throne, took off his
royal robes, covered himself with sackcloth and sat down in the dust.

—Jonah 3:5–6

To call it remarkable is to miss the breadth. Nowhere in biblical or secular history has one message produced a greater harvest. The apostle Paul would say that the city's "sorrow led [them] to repentance" (2 Cor. 7:9). The populace believed God—and Nineveh then was a metropolitan population pushing a million! So moved was the king that he issued the following proclamation:

"By the decree of the king and his nobles: Do not let any man or
beast, herd or flock, taste anything; do not let them eat or drink.
But let man and beast be covered with sackcloth. Let everyone call
urgently on God. Let them give up their evil ways and their vio-
lence. Who knows? God may yet relent and with compassion turn
from his fierce anger so that we will not perish."

—Jonah 3:7–9

The greatest miracle in the book of Jonah is not that a man was swallowed by a fish and lived to tell about it. The greatest miracle is the wholesale repentance of the Ninevites!

Praise

And did the Lord "relent, and with compassion turn from His fierce anger," as the king and his nobles hoped? The Word states,

When God saw what they did and how they turned from their evil
ways, he had compassion and did not bring upon them the destruc-
tion he had threatened.

—Jonah 3:10

That's mercy. When God saw their deeds—the fruit of repentance, something that a saving faith will always produce (see James 1:4; Matt. 3:7–8)—He had compassion.[1] God has never taken pleasure in the death of the wicked (see Ezek. 33:11), and He still doesn't. When people see themselves as sinners and trust in God's only provision, made plain in our times to be Jesus Christ (see John 3:16), what a delight it is to the heart of our Lord. All heaven rejoices in praise. So it was when Nineveh believed God—a symphony of praise filling the halls above.

But Jonah? "[He] was greatly displeased and became angry" (Jonah 4:1). The word *angry* means in the original "to burn." Indeed, Jonah was so hot he prayed, "O LORD, take away my life, for it is better for me to die than to live" (v. 3).

No praise and no desire to live—a coincidence? Not exactly. A smooth seam joins a lack of praise and a desire to quit.

In the daytime, stick your thumb up close to one eye and, with the other eye shut, look skyward. Now with your thumb block out the sun. How about that—you hid old Sol!

It doesn't take an astronomer to figure out that the sun disappeared because of perspective, not actual fact. Nobody can really hide an object that's 864,000 miles in diameter. But let's just suppose that on the basis of the darkness caused by your thumb's close proximity to your eye, you choose to make some decisions, like putting on your pj's and heading to bed. Faulty perspectives lead to suspect decisions.

The person who is unable to praise God—the Alpha and the Omega—lives life from the wrong perspective. The eternal Son always shines, and ascribing glory to Him is simply acknowledging that it is so. "Shine, Jesus, shine!" To deny through a lack of praise that He is present in your ministry is to live with a thumb in your spiritual eye. When that happens, watch out. Pajamas, here we come!

Taught but Not Caught

Jonah's spiritual plight was indeed severe. At a minimum, three "thumbs" blocked out the light and contributed to his decision to quit. The first "thumb" was an unteachable spirit.

[Jonah] prayed to the LORD, "O LORD, is this not what I said when I was still at home? That is why I was so quick to flee to

Tarshish. I knew that you are a gracious and compassionate God,
slow to anger and abounding in love, a God who relents from send-
ing calamity."

—Jonah 4:2

And that's just what God did when it came to Nineveh. In grace, compassion, love, and slowness to anger, He backed off. And Jonah knew that God would do that, because he knew that was the way God is. Whether from others, history, or the Lord Himself, Jonah had learned much about God.

But, oh, Jonah was unteachable! It was that same grace, compassion, love, and slowness to anger that got Jonah back up and running, that put him into dry threads, that gave him a hope. It was the Lord who was "gracious and compassionate" to him. It was the Lord who was "slow to anger and abounding in love" toward him. It was the Lord who relented "from sending calamity" upon him. Jonah knew about God, but he didn't know God for himself. He knew about Him for others. He knew about Him for the Ninevites. He knew about Him for sermons. He knew about Him for ministry decisions. But he did not know Him for himself. The storm, the toss overboard, the big fish—and living to tell about it—and Jonah did not learn for himself. An unteachable spirit.

In Japan in the 1800s there lived a Zen master by the name of Nan-In. One day he invited one of his students to his home. After they had chatted for a while, the old man asked, "May I serve you some tea?"

"Yes, thank you," replied the disciple, and they both sat down on the floor at a low table. Nan-In set a teacup in front of the student and began to pour. He talked while he poured the tea, all the while his eyes latched onto the pupil's face. The young man was so involved in what the master said that at first he didn't notice that the cup overflowed. Nan-In just kept pouring. Finally, the student interrupted, "Stop! You have overfilled the cup!"

Nan-In stopped and smiled. Then he said, "Yes, the cup is overfull, and you, my friend, are like this cup—so full of your own thoughts and ideas that I can't teach you any wisdom. You must first empty the cup."[2]

Was that not Jonah? Could that be us? So full of ourselves right now that we can't be taught that same grace, compassion, love, and slowness to anger that God extends to those to whom we minister? Unteachable people accumulate knowledge about God—for others, for their ministries—but somehow they don't grasp the knowledge of God for themselves. They have unteachable spirits.

Here's a suggestion to guard against this thumb in your spiritual eye and, if it's already there, a way to remove it. Meditate on what you know about the Lord before Him. With an open Bible, pencil, and paper, write it out. Not for a seminary professor, but for yourself in His presence. You know what will happen? Praise. Praise that influences for good the decision-making process.

The truth "God is faithful," for example, is reiterated throughout the Word. We know it for those to whom we minister—in times of trial, in times of grief, in times of confusion, and in times when it looks as if the bottom is about to drop out. We know that for those we care for God is faithful. We share it with them. We try to point to times in the past when it was evident to them. We show in the Word that it's been evident for others. God is still the same God, and His faithfulness will again be evident for them.

But do we do the same for ourselves? It's so easy to think that because we preach it, we believe it. For there to be praise from us, truths about God for ourselves must be meditated on before the Lord. In our times of trial. In our times of grief. In our times of confusion. In times when it looks as if the bottom is about to drop out from under us. When faced with the unexpected, we must learn those truths about God all over again— fresh for ourselves on each occasion. We cannot afford to assume that because we know it for others, we know it for ourselves. Because those truths about God are infinite, there's always more of it to know.

"Father, this means that You cannot be anything but faithful to me right now—no matter what others say or what my feelings say. You are faithful. You will see me through. I've seen it in my past. I've seen it in others. I've seen it in those to whom I minister. I've seen it in the Word. It's tough because things around me have changed, but You have not. Father, great is Thy faithfulness."

Praise. Worship. Continue daily to know God for ourselves. Where are you? If you have not moved beyond knowing *about* God, then it's no surprise that you want to quit. Facts alone do not satisfy. They're like sipping from an empty watercooler. The mechanism to quench our thirst is there but not the water. Because both parts are necessary, a cooler without the water will not quench your thirst.

Knowledge about God for others is not enough. Oh, for sure, the facts are necessary, but they're not enough. There must be the water. We must take the truth—His grace, His compassion, His slowness to anger, His abounding love, His faithfulness, everything that He has revealed Himself to be—for ourselves and meditate on it before Him. Once that is done, praise will come. It might be slow at first. We might not even recognize it as praise at first. But it will come. A teachable person will get beyond knowing about God, will know Him for him or herself, and will overflow in worship to God.

An unteachable believer won't. That individual is already convinced that he or she knows all about God and will proceed to tell Him so—and in the process will make one of those decisions that looks so right but prove so wrong.

Is That So?

Jonah was teed off because God refused to fuel the flames of hell with Mr. and Mrs. Nineveh along with all of their little Ninevites. Jonah's rationale? Nineveh was the capital city of Assyria, the greatest enemy of Jonah's own countrymen. Why offer them a second chance? "Torch them, God; do away with Israel's threat. Fry them to a crisp!"

But they weren't fried. Not even sautéed. And that was too much for the prophet. The people in Jonah's country lived for the day when Assyria would get zapped. Would Jonah return home as the Moses of Nineveh? No way. Better to die. So when it became obvious that what Jonah wanted and what happened were not the same, Jonah asked God to play the grim reaper: "Now, O LORD, take away my life, for it is better for me to die than to live" (Jonah 4:3). The second "thumb"? Presumption.

In 1965 in the town of Arles, France, a man named Andre-Francois Raffray, age forty-seven, made a real-estate deal with a ninety-year-old widow, Jeanne Calment. The contract called for Mr. Raffray to pay Mrs. Calment five hundred dollars a month until her death, at which time her apartment would become his property. This sort of arrangement is common in France, because in a country where housing is difficult to obtain, it benefits both elderly people living on fixed incomes and buyers.

It didn't work out so well for Mr. Raffray, however. Mrs. Calment (as of this writing) has become the world's oldest living person. Now more than one hundred and twenty years old, she outlived Mr. Raffray. When he died at age seventy-seven in 1995, he had already paid $184,000 for an apartment in which he had never been able to live. Not only that but also his heirs are bound by the contract to continue paying Mrs. Calment until she dies.[3] Presumption. It can get you into all kinds of trouble.

It did Jonah. Maybe it was the storm. Maybe it was surviving the man-eating fish. Maybe it was God's insistence that he go. Something convinced Jonah that he was God's messenger of Nineveh's destruction. What a letdown for Jonah when Nineveh repented and God relented! Presumption.

Believers exhibit all kinds of negative behavior—resentment, cynicism, bitterness—because at some time in their pasts they were convinced that God was going to do one thing and He did something totally different. Because of this, those Christians have become acidic. Why? Their pride has been hurt.

And that's all presumption is—pride. We think that we have cornered the market on God. To us, His ways are predictable; His thoughts are scrutable. But when reality confounds us, we discover that the Lord is past finding out. Then we will either confess our sin of presumption, or, like Jonah, turn sour. Remember, spiritual maturity is not characterized by the ability to explain all that's going on; it's marked by a growing capacity to respond properly to what we encounter.

When you walk down the sidewalk, do you analyze why a car barrels down a driveway right in front of you? No. You take evasive action. If you come to a street corner and discover that the pedestrian "walk" sign is out of order, do you question Providence and try to determine the significance behind what you found? No. You look both ways and cross the street.

Things happen to us in ministry that do not meet our expectations and that are inexplicable. The more we grow in the Lord, the more we will realize this fact. Our concern, however, is not to explain the unexpected but to respond properly to it, to maneuver as safely as possible around, over, or even through the things that lie in our paths.

And praising God? It will come. The fact that God is unexplainable and brings about the unexpected can only bow the knee of a maturing believer. I am not awed by an arrow shot into the air. But I am impressed every time I watch a space shuttle launch. The technology and engineering are beyond me.

We bow the knee to God because He is beyond us in both His person and His ways. Mystery enshrouds Him. Praise is thus His due. Only the presumptuous would think otherwise.

Thank You, Lord

Presumptuous to the hilt—that was Jonah. So much so that he "went out and sat down at a place east of the city. There he made himself a shelter, sat in its shade and waited to see what would happen to the city" (Jonah 4:5). And why did he set up shop in the suburbs? After God had spared the city, Jonah voted for Nineveh's destruction, and now he hoped for a recount; he had prayed that God would reconsider and vote in the affirmative, too. While he sat it out, though, Jonah was pleasantly surprised:

> Then the LORD God provided a vine and made it grow up over Jonah to give shade for his head to ease his discomfort, and Jonah was very happy about the vine.
>
> —Jonah 4:6

Do we hear "Thank you, Lord"?

> But at dawn the next day God provided a worm, which chewed the vine so that it withered. When the sun rose, God provided a scorching east wind, and the sun blazed on Jonah's head.
>
> —Jonah 4:7–8

How about "Lord, I'm eternally grateful that I can trust You for You do all things well"?

> *He grew faint. He wanted to die, and said, "It would be better for me to die than to live." But God said to Jonah, "Do you have a right to be angry about the vine?" "I do," he said. "I am angry enough to die." But the Lord said, "You have been concerned about this vine, though you did not tend it or make it grow. It sprang up overnight and died overnight. But Nineveh has more than a hundred and twenty thousand people who cannot tell their right hand from their left, and many cattle as well. Should I not be concerned about that great city?"*
>
> —Jonah 4:8–11

Do we hear "Lord, forgive me. I was wrong! Thank You for showing such compassion toward both me and Nineveh, especially the toddlers"?

No? Three strikes on Jonah and he's out.

To be fair, we don't know what, if anything, Jonah said; the book ends at verse eleven. But it's ominous.

We do know this: nowhere in the last half of this story does Jonah stop and express gratitude toward God for anything that He did. In fact, only once do we find the prophet even joyful: "And Jonah was very happy about the vine" (4:6). No wonder he could not praise God. An ungrateful spirit had obscured His presence—a third "thumb" in the spiritual eye of the prophet.

The writer to the Hebrews says, "Through Him then, let us continually offer up a sacrifice of praise to God, that is, the fruit of lips that give thanks to His name" (Heb. 13:15 NASB), thereby linking gratitude with praise. Genuine worship of God is always synonymous with a grateful heart. Otherwise, whatever is offered up is somewhat less than authentic praise.

Have you thanked God today for how He's using where you are and what you struggle against to achieve His ends, even though you don't understand it? If we really believe that we have a sovereign Lord who "causes all things to work together for good" (Rom. 8:28 NASB), then 1 Thessalonians 5:18 is a reasonable command: "Give thanks in all circumstances, for this is God's will for you in Christ Jesus."

Give thanks? For the sin that's tearing up my ministry?

No. That God is able to take such a situation and use it to accomplish His purpose.

For the lies that are being framed to destroy my reputation?

No. That God employs such settings to fulfill His goals.

For the pain this ministry is causing my family?

No. That God will see to it that the pain is not wasted in their lives.

The fact that our Lord rules over all, never changing even though our surroundings do, is the basis for a believer's gratitude. We thank Him for Himself and His ways—no matter our lot. That makes 1 Thessalonians 5:18 come alive.

Missionary Ruth Kilbourne first shared the following true account. During the Korean conflict, a young Korean woman was pregnant. On Christmas, the labor pains started, and she walked through the snow toward the home of a missionary, whom she knew would help. As she neared a bridge, the birth pains became so strong that she could go no farther. So the young woman crawled under the bridge and there, under its trestles, gave birth to a perfect baby boy. It was Christmas night.

Having nothing except the heavy clothes that she was wearing, the young woman removed them and wrapped her tiny son like a cocoon. Then, finding a discarded piece of gunny sack, she pulled it over herself and lay exhausted in the snow beside her baby.

The next morning the missionary at the compound got in her jeep to take a Christmas basket to a needy family. She had just crossed the bridge when her jeep sputtered to a stop, out of gas. As she walked across the bridge toward the compound, she heard a faint cry beneath her. Crawling under the bridge to investigate, she found the tiny baby, warm and hungry. Beside him was the young mother, frozen to death.

The missionary took the baby home and cared for him as her own. As he grew, the boy often asked the missionary to tell him how she had found him. One Christmas day, his twelfth birthday, he asked the missionary to take him to his mother's grave. When she did, the boy requested that she wait at a distance while he went on to the grave. Standing at the grave, he bowed his head and began to weep. The missionary watched in astonishment as he began to remove his clothing, piece by piece, and lay it across his mother's grave. It was bitterly cold and the missionary thought, *He surely won't take off all of his clothing. He'll freeze.*

But the young boy stripped himself of every piece of clothing, placing the clothes on the grave, and knelt there shivering in the snow. As the missionary stepped toward him to help him dress again, she heard him cry out to the mother whom he never knew, "Were you colder than this for me, my mother?" Then he broke down and wept bitterly.

There ought to be something where you are or in what you do that moves you to say *thank you.* If not in the people, if not in the results, if not in the sense of satisfaction, surely in what the Lord has done for you and for those to whom you minister. What He suffered for you and me, for those to whom we minister. What He was to suffer for Jonah, for those to whom he ministered—surely that's enough to bow the head and knee in heartfelt thanks.

Friend, if it isn't, get the thumb out of your eye.

Do You Praise God . . . Now?

Are you packing your ministerial bags with a song in your heart? I'm sorry, I didn't catch what you said. You're packing and there's no song? There's little, if any, praise welling up from within to your God? Is that what you said?

If that's so, maybe you do have some thumbs in front of your face. If you are unable to praise God where you are, and where you are is where God meant for you to be, then it's a sure sign that your bags are out too soon. Jonah's consistent lack of praise at Nineveh and his decision twice to quit on life is not something to ignore. Where there is no true worship of God there is no interest in the will of God.

If you cannot bow the knee right now on the ground where God has placed you, then you have no business looking for greener pastures; you will not bow the knee there, either. Only when there is an artesian well of genuine praise to our God can a committed believer seriously consider quitting when things are hard.

"Wait, Blaine. I thought that the whole point of this book has been *don't quit when facing difficulty.*"

No. According to Scripture, hardship is sometimes a valid reason for making a change. God does use pain to direct us to the next station in His plan for our lives. For the early church in Jerusalem, God used the stoning of Stephen to maneuver the infant body beyond the borders of the city. Luke tells us in the book of Acts that on the very day that Stephen was stoned, "a great persecution broke out against the church at Jerusalem, and all except the apostles were scattered throughout Judea and Samaria" (Acts 8:1). For the majority of the early church, God used hardship to reveal His will—which was to leave Jerusalem and move on. But the apostles? They were to stay—proof that, even when people share circumstances in common, God does not have the same plan for each.

Again, what is crucial is the atmosphere in which the decision to stay or to leave is made: problem plus praise or problem minus praise. When, as the result of Stephen's stoning, persecution broke out for the early church, both those who left and those who stayed were already accustomed to giving praise under fire (e.g., see Acts 4:23–31; 5:40–42.). It was their hallmark. They always saw God's hand in their circumstances. With hearts like that, hardship for some meant that it was best to leave—and to do it in God's will—whereas for others the same hardship meant that it was best to stay—and to do it in God's will. Each was able to discern God's pleasure because of that drive to please the Lord.

So the first question is not "Are you to leave your difficult surroundings?" The answer to that question could be either yes or no, depending on God's will for you in that particular setting. The first question is, as it was with Jonah, "Have thumbs obscured God's light and affected your decision-making process?"

If they have not, then the desire to move might be of Him—or it might not. Either way, if your heart can praise the Lord where you are right now, whatever His will, you will know when you need to know.

But if your praise has been affected to the extent that it is only mechanical—just parroting words—or possibly even nonexistent, then quitting is like running a red light.

Only a foolish person would do that. Only a Jonah.

EPILOGUE

Plastered across a teenager's T-shirt was this statement: "If you are losing the game, change the rules." *Before You Quit: When Ministry Is Not What You Thought* is a reminder: Although it might seem that you are losing the game, don't change the rules.

And what are God's rules for His servants? Paul instructed Timothy to "pursue righteousness, godliness, faith, love, endurance" (1 Tim. 6:11). These ends—even the last one—are not negotiable. We are to pursue a life that is willing to endure anything as long as it is our Lord's plan for us.

Will we always score 100 percent? No. There is yet to be a mortal to receive 100 percent on each and every decision. In this world, a perfect score is impossible; no one will get an A on content. But let's not go to the other extreme. Just because God knows that we are not perfect in all of our decisions does not imply that God expects total failures. We are to "approve the things that are excellent, in order to be sincere and blameless until the day of Christ" (Phil. 1:10 NASB).

Our son Brian, like most kids at age two, developed into quite a chatterbox. He worked hard at pronouncing his words. Still, "little" was *yittle,* "thank you" was *tattoom* and "peanut butter" was *peabubby.*

Perfect?

No.

Sincere and without blame?

Totally.

God's children are no different. Although there will be no A's on content, there will be A's on effort. We are to endure all that is a part of God's will for our lives. Sure, not every decision will prove to be perfect. But if our goal is to persevere within the will of God, then we cannot be faulted for lack of sincerity and blamelessness. *Perseverance* is not some archaic King James word. It is a quality for which, if necessary, God wants us to die.

Winston Churchill's credo was,

> Never give in.
> Never give in.
> Never.
> Never.
> Never.

Whatever God has for you, you be the same.

> Never give in.
> Never give in.
> Never.
> Never.
> Never.

If God wants you stay where you are, persevere. If God wants you to leave, then you *have* persevered. Either way, don't quit, remembering who said,

> *"To him who overcomes, I will give the right to sit with me on my throne, just as I overcame and sat down with my Father on his throne."*
>
> —Revelation 3:21

NOTES

Introduction

1. "Prayer Requests," *Aim International,* summer 1988.
2. Hugh Steven, *A Thousand Trails* (Huntington Beach, Calif.: Wycliffe Bible Translators, 1984), 76. Biography of Cameron Townsend 1917–1919.
3. Told by Pastor David Wilkinson, Trinity Presbyterian Church, Orville, Calif., "Building Blocks: How to Avoid Them," *Leadership* 5, no. 1 (winter 1984): 116.

Chapter 2: Ministry Under Siege

1. The phrase *forced out* is used to describe both terminations and intense pressure to resign.
2. John C. LaRue Jr., "Forced Exits: A Too-Common Ministry Hazard," *Your Church,* March-April 1996, 72. Nine hundred ninety-nine surveys were mailed randomly to U.S. pastors who subscribe to *Leadership, Christianity Today,* and *Your Church.* A total of 593 pastors responded (a 59 percent response rate). Results are considered accurate with a sample of this size to within plus or minus 4 percentage points 95 percent of the time.
3. Ibid.
4. James Dobson, *Focus on the Family Newsletter,* February 1997.
5. True story, but names have been changed.
6. Adapted from Paul Harvey Jr., "Excuses, Excuses!" in *More of Paul Harvey's The Rest of the Story* (New York: William Morrow & Co., Inc., 1980), 3–5.

7. Eugene H. Peterson, "The Business of Making Saints," *Leadership,* spring 1997, 28.
8. Ibid.
9. Stephen Pile, "The Greatest Mathematical Error," in *The Book of Heroic Failure* (New York: Ballantine, 1986). From InfoSearch Illustration Files.

Chapter 4: No Delight, No Go

1. Chuck Colson, "Living the Faith," *Christian Life Magazine,* January 1984, 71.
2. J. Wallace Hamilton, *Ride the Wild Horses* (Westwood, N.J.: Fleming H. Revell, 1952), 76.

Chapter 5: Who's Calling the Shots?

1. Karen Lewis, "The Men Behind the Three-Piece Suits," *In Other Words,* December 1982, 4.

Chapter 8: Empty

1. True story, but the name and setting have been changed to protect the guilty.

Chapter 9: Second Thoughts

1. Joe Garagiola, *It's Anybody's Ballgame* (Chicago: Contemporary Books, 1988), 305.
2. Bernie May, "Climbing on Course," *In Other Words,* February–March 1982, 8.

Chapter 10: Cost Audit

1. Haddon Robinson, "Whom Do You Fear?" *Our Daily Bread,* 9 November 1997.

Chapter 11: Thumbs

1. When the text says, "God saw their deeds," it does not mean that the people were saved by their good works. These were not deeds of merit but evidence of a moral change within. Salvation (under both the Old and New Testaments) is impossible to earn. "For by grace you have been saved through faith; and that not of yourselves, it is the gift of God; not as a result of works, that no one should boast" (Eph. 2:8–9 NASB).
2. Roger Van Oech, *A Whack on the Side of the Head* (New York: Warner Books, 1983), 10.
3. Steve Abbott, "To Illustrate," *Leadership,* summer 1996, 65.